room rescues

Jane Burdon

room rescues

decorating solutions for awkward spaces

RYLAND
PETERS
& SMALL
LONDON NEW YORK

This book is dedicated to Patrick

SENIOR DESIGNER Sally Powell
SENIOR EDITOR Henrietta Heald
PICTURE RESEARCH Emily Westlake
PRODUCTION Patricia Harrington
ART DIRECTOR Gabriella Le Grazie
PUBLISHING DIRECTOR Alison Starling

First published in the United Kingdom in 2005 by
Ryland Peters & Small
20–21 Jockey's Fields
London WC1R 4BW
www.rylandpeters.com

10 9 8 7 6 5 4 3 2 1

ISBN 1 84172 801 2

A CIP record for this book is available from the British Library.

Printed and bound in China.

Key: ph= photographer, a=above, b=below, r=right, l=left, c=centre.

Front jacket above left ph Ray Main/a loft in London designed by Circus
Architects; above centre ph Polly Wreford/Clare Nash's house in London;
above right ph Chris Everard/Michael Nathenson's house in London; centre
ph Debi Treloar/Kristiina Ratia and Jeff Gocke's family home in Norwalk,
Connecticut; below left ph Chris Everard/Jo Warman – Interior Concepts;
centre right ph Jan Baldwin/architect Joseph Dirand's apartment in Paris;
below right ph Chris Everard/the London apartment of the Sheppard Day
Design Partnership.
Back jacket left ph Jan Baldwin/Sophie Eadie's family home in London; centre
ph Ray Main/client's residence, East Hampton, New York, designed by ZG
DESIGN; right ph Chris Everard/photographer Guy Hills' house in London
designed by Joanna Rippon and Maria Speake of Retrouvius.

introduction

Many of the beautiful coffee-table books that inspire us to decorate our homes imply that all rooms are light-filled spaces with high ceilings and fantastic architectural details. In reality, most houses and flats include at least one awkward space such as a narrow hallway or a tiny study that struggles to double as a spare bedroom. The good news is that working around a problem can often result in a space that is far more cohesive and full of impact than a room where there has been no necessity to try so hard. This book offers clear, practical advice to help you to make the most of all the rooms in your home regardless of their imperfections.

The most powerful tools in tackling any problem are knowledge, confidence and an ability to see the positive as well as the negative aspects of an issue. The aim of *Room Rescues* is to arm you with all three, so that you can enjoy the process of decorating your home.

Each chapter is dedicated to a specific type of 'problem' room – for example, a room that is small, dark or narrow – and begins with a Golden Rules section setting out dos and don'ts when trying to realize the potential of your space. Extensively illustrated Solutions pages show inspiring examples of creative solutions that have been used in real homes. Decorating Palettes offer suggestions for colour schemes, patterns and styles that will work really well in your space.

Finally, since problems often come in twos or threes, the book concludes with a section showing how to mix and match solutions to solve the puzzle of rooms that have more than one trouble spot, whether they are small and dark or cold and bland.

what's your problem?

It is no accident that the first chapter of *Room Rescues* tackles small rooms. Making space stretch further is a priority for many people, and fitting belongings into undersized rooms is never easy. Thinking Big covers choosing furniture, reducing clutter and creating adequate storage (if there is such a thing). Next, Broadening Your Outlook demonstrates how to open up narrow and claustrophobic spaces. Hallways in particular are prone to being skinny, and often all that's needed to improve their looks is a strong focal point or better lighting.

Oddly shaped or out-of-proportion rooms can also be transformed into charming and original spaces if you know how to set about it. Changing Shape provides solutions for irregular walls, uneven floors and awkward angles. If low ceilings are getting you down, discover some eye-deceiving tricks in Aiming High.

As explained in Lightening Up, there is no need to put up with a gloomy interior. This chapter describes how to maximize light by choosing the right window treatments and clever use of colour and artificial lighting. The way you choose to dress your windows is also crucial for rooms that are overlooked. Creating Privacy considers how to deter glances from passers-by and the options for screening off a section of an open-plan room temporarily for working or relaxing. There are also tips for introducing harmony into shared children's bedrooms and using plants to create secluded spaces.

Adding Character shows how to inject extra interest into rooms that lack architectural detail or bland spaces that have lost their way in a sea of uninspiring furniture and decor. Don't worry if a bold statement or an eclectic look isn't what you're after. The chapter also shows how to use fabrics and accessories to introduce texture or create a soft, layered look. If you have a room that looks or feels chilly and unwelcoming, it's time to turn up the heat. Warming Up will show you how to choose suitable colour schemes and textures along with the right flooring and furnishings. Finally, if your home is feeling slightly past it, turn to the Giving Refreshment chapter. Discovering how to minimize the impact of dated windows or fireplaces, or going with the flow and introducing a deliberately retro feel, will instantly turn a tired room into a fresh, uplifting space.

clearing the decks

Clutter does no favours to any interior, and it can compound the problems of an awkward space. Start your room makeover with a clean slate by sorting through surplus furniture and little-used belongings. Take a leaf out of the book of Arts and Crafts designer William Morris and 'have nothing in your house that you do not know to be useful or believe to be beautiful'. Donate unwanted items to charity or raise cash and have some fun at a car-boot sale.

If you can't decide whether or not to let particular possessions go, try the cardboard-box technique. Pack everything you are unsure about in a box and leave it in a garage or loft for six months. If you don't miss any of the items, you will know that it is time to part company with them. Keep remaining keepsakes fresh by rotating displays regularly. Paper clutter can be kept under control by paying bills promptly or setting up accounts online. Place a good-looking filing tray and a wastepaper bin near places where you open mail and empty both before they are ready to overflow. A good clear-out will make you feel on top of things and allow you to address your problem room with a clear head.

a plan of action

Once you have finished disposing of clutter, take a long, hard look at the space. Decide which features can be accentuated and identify the trouble spots that you want to play down. Try to be both realistic and flexible at this stage, and be willing to lower your expectations when necessary. Is a room really too small, for example, or are your plans to combine a study and spare bedroom overambitious? Are you stubbornly holding on to a favourite pair of heavy-lined curtains, even though they block out too much light?

Groundwork isn't a waste of time, so don't simply resort to a paintbrush at the first opportunity. The more research you do before starting to decorate, the happier you will be with the result. Look around your friends' homes and shamelessly steal schemes that appeal to you. If a room feels good to be in, try to work out why so that you can replicate the effect at home. Window-shop for ideas in stores that are above your budget, then look around for cheaper alternatives elsewhere. Mood boards are enjoyable to make, and will help you to envisage the look of a finished room. Collect paint colour cards and fabric swatches along with pages torn from magazines and anything else that inspires you, and mix them together to create a style-setting collage.

In contrast with other books on home decorating, *Room Rescues* does not attempt to dictate any one style in which to decorate your home. Like people, rooms come in all shapes and sizes, and some of them are easier to work with than others. Combining the suggestions and solutions in this book with your own tastes and preferences will allow you to create relaxed and personal interiors. After all, feeling comfortable at home is one of life's fundamental pleasures.

We all crave the large, airy rooms featured in interiors magazines, which promise relaxation, sophistication and tranquillity without the real-life tangles of TV wires and cluttered surfaces. So how is it possible to recreate those glamorous scenes in much smaller spaces? To start by looking on the bright side, small rooms are undeniably

thinking big

cosy, which can be a plus in a bedroom. Think about reallocating the rooms in your home to suit their proportions better – and you may find that you don't have a size problem after all. Also, pint-sized rooms require their owners to be disciplined about what goes in them. This may not seem like an advantage, but it is refreshing to live as simply as possible, free from extraneous objects.

Editing the contents of a small room is crucial. This applies not only to junk mail and old birthday cards but also to furniture. Weed out unnecessary side-tables; replace bulky armchairs with neat tub seats; and remove the dressing table if you don't use it. Consider investing in hard-working, dual-function, stackable or stowable pieces.

The next task is to find a home for everything that's left. In kitchens, invest in mini and slimline appliances that leave room for additional storage, and include drawers at the bottom of kitchen units, behind the kick plates. Exploit vertical space by creating floor-to-ceiling storage or hanging cooking utensils from the ceiling or walls. Arrange books by height, and add extra shelves to bookcases. Put racks on the backs of wardrobe doors for storing shoes and accessories. Fit sockets inside cupboards so that you can stack away computer equipment. Set radiators into alcoves or install underfloor heating and reclaim wall space. The aim is to use every under-stair, above-fridge, top-of-wardrobe scrap of storage potential.

Optical tricks and illusions can often help. For example, a colourful woven rug or a low coffee table decorated with one or two interesting objects creates a focal point in the middle of a room, taking attention away from its edges – and its limited dimensions. Being able to glimpse the floor under pieces of furniture reduces their apparent bulk. A bedroom will look bigger if a divan is replaced by a footed base and a mattress of the same size, and a bathroom with a claw-footed bath looks bigger than one with a boxed-in version.

○ lighten walls

Paint or paper your walls with pale tints of 'receding' colours such as blue, green or lilac. Avoid 'advancing' colours such as red or orange.

○ 'borrow' space

Blur boundaries by continuing both wall colour and neutral flooring into neighbouring rooms. Keep internal doors open to allow views of other spaces. Dress windows simply, and trim any plants and shrubs outside them to open up the view.

golden rules
FOR SMALL SPACES

○ exploit shine

Use mirrors and other reflective surfaces to bounce light around a room and create new vistas. Try adding mirrored tiles to a sink splashback, painting a wall in a glossy finish or installing a marble or limestone floor in a bathroom or kitchen.

○ banish clutter

Pare down furniture to a minimum to create extra floor space and a clean, uncluttered look. Choose convertible or stowable pieces. Minimize solid shapes by investing in furniture with legs. Take inspiration from the ingenious designs found in caravans, boats and barges.

○ think eye-level impact

Declutter the zone that is at eye-level on entering a room. Don't fix wall-mounted units or cabinets on the wall facing the entrance, for example. Hang several small pictures in a group rather than scattering them around the walls.

○ broaden horizons

Encourage the eye to scan the longest sweep of space by putting a long, low bench along one wall, for example, or installing a row of halogen spotlights that continue into another area. Replace tall, skinny bookcases with broader ones, or group several together to 'fatten them up'.

○ rehang doors

Alter the perception of space by rehanging a door so that it opens the opposite way. Consider swapping traditional doors with sliding ones – or getting rid of them all together.

○ place furniture carefully

Keep furniture at right angles to walls. Set tables and chairs slightly away from the walls so you can see space beyond them. Try to blur edges and corners by strategically placing furniture – if the eye can see every angle, the brain quickly deduces that the room is tiny.

○ create a focal point

Make a central statement to draw the eye towards the middle of the room and distract attention away from its edges – and its limited dimensions.

○ avoid pattern overload

Ban wallpaper or furnishing fabric with a large repeat. Stick to small motifs on walls or furniture (not both), and work with only one or two designs. Papers with a small square grid or tiling effect make a room look bigger.

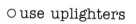

○ use uplighters

Downlighters are required for tasks such as reading, cooking and putting on make-up, but, if you want to add height and distract attention from a room's dimensions, install uplighters that cast beams of vertical light.

1

2

solutions
FOR SMALL SPACES

1 Sliding doors are a wonderful solution for spaces that are too small to accommodate the opening of traditional doors. Here, frosted-glass room dividers offer clean-lined, understated elegance, and allow privacy when needed in an essentially open-plan space.

2 When space is at a premium, a little lateral thinking can go a long way. This beautifully tiled bathroom has effectively been divided into two skinny sections placed end to end, occupying a mere sliver of space. Sliding doors add to the sleek contemporary space-saving style.

3 Open-plan living areas make good use of limited floor space and are excellent for entertaining, but not everyone wants to stare at piles of washing-up while eating supper. The simple solution is a kitchen built on a single wall, and a pair of neat sliding doors that screen off the area in an instant.

4 If you have limited floor space, think vertically. In this bedroom, a pair of vintage filing cabinets serve as both bedside tables and storage. The bed's tall metal headboard complements both the cabinets' proportions and their utilitarian look.

5 Paring down small rooms to let them breathe doesn't mean stripping a home of its character. Although the rooms in this apartment are filled with books and antique furniture, wide-open doorways provide views to other areas, effectively creating an illusion of space and preventing a claustrophobic feel.

6 The rooms of this diminutive house have been furnished as simply as possible to allow clear unadulterated outdoor views. Neutral walls and flooring and well-positioned furniture lead the eye to gloriously oversized and undressed windows.

7 A lucky find in a salvage yard, this vast antique mirror doubles the apparent size of an entrance hall. Mirrors greatly enhance the feeling of space, and bounce large amounts of light into a room: the effect here is positively palatial.

8 Fitted units work better than freestanding pieces in small kitchens. Where possible, choose wider than average cabinets, which will make your room look broader. Illuminating the areas above and below the units creates a 'floating' effect, suggesting continuing space.

9 Simple tricks can be used effectively to blur boundaries between rooms. In this small apartment, wide-open doors, along with uniform flooring and décor throughout, transform three compact rooms into one glorious salon.

10 Small spaces look best if their contents are scaled down and in proportion to the room, but throwing an oversized object into the mix can add an element of individuality and fun to your space. In this room, a huge clock found in a junk shop holds pride of place above a work station.

4

5

11

11 Inspired by the humble serving hatch, internal 'windows' give small rooms a welcome outlook into adjoining areas. These openings cleverly mimic both the rounded 1960s-style kitchen cabinets and the curves of the dining-room table, visually linking the two spaces.

12 Painting skirting boards the same colour as your floor will subtly suggest a larger surface area by blurring the edges of the room. The use of soft grey for all the room's woodwork gives interest to an otherwise neutral space.

13 The principle of painting skirting boards the same colour as the floor has been taken a step further in this hallway. White paint in a high-gloss finish has been used to bounce the maximum amount of light into a narrow passage.

14 Sofas and chairs upholstered in pale, neutral shades tend to work best in small spaces, but you may need, or prefer, to work with what you already have. Soften the impact of solid dark shapes with throws and cushions.

15 Freestanding kitchens can look charming and original, but in a tiny room they waste precious storage space and can give a cluttered impression. Choose integral appliances and hide them behind unfussy doors to create a uniform effect that encourages the eye to sweep across the space.

16

17

18

16 Acknowledged as a necessary evil, radiators use up valuable space and are visually messy. One solution is to have them fitted into alcoves.

17 Glass walls are a good choice for compact rooms. They seem less solid than conventional bricks and plaster, and more substantial than screens. In this flat, a frosted partition screens off a corridor, while allowing light to fill the space.

18 Mini black and white tiles help to make the floor look bigger in a compact kitchen. Pans and utensils hanging from the wall and ceiling are practical, decorative and, above all, draw the eye towards the vertical.

19 Another way to deal with radiators is to conceal them behind sleek radiator covers that blend with the surroundings.

20 Floor-to-ceiling storage is a must for small spaces. Choose flat-fronted cupboards, dress them with minimal door furniture, and paint them the same colour as the walls – and you will hardly notice that they are there.

21 A large see-through coffee table sits happily with an oversized mirror, eclectic shelving and a neutral sofa. If space is tight, a transparent table or chair made of glass, Perspex or acrylic will prevent your room looking crammed, and can be easily combined with other materials.

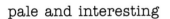

pale and interesting

Pale colours make surfaces appear larger because they contain lots of white, which reflects light. Choosing shades from the cooler end of the spectrum will exaggerate this effect, since these colours naturally recede, making the walls seem farther away. Note that combined shades recede even more than pure hues, so a soft grey-blue will make a room look even larger than a clear blue of the same intensity.

decorating palettes
FOR SMALL SPACES

tone on tone

Confining a decorative scheme to a single neutral colour will maximize a room's proportions but may look rather unexciting. You can inject interest into neutral walls, fabrics and accessories by incorporating several tones of the same colour into the scheme. Graduating colour from wall to wall is also a subtle way to add an impression of depth to small spaces.

white with bright splashes

Pure, clean white can be used to flood light into small rooms and disguise their limited dimensions. Add splashes of bright, saturated colour to create a focal point and prevent the room from looking too stark or monastic. Shop around for a pure white that contains no hint of another colour (brilliant white contains blue brighteners that can have a cold effect in some lights).

repeat if desired

Pattern introduces individuality and character into a decorative scheme, but it needs to be treated with care in small spaces. The key to success is to keep to an essentially pale colour palette and add just a little of what you love. Give interest to a cream sofa with gloriously patterned cushions, or paper one wall with a small floral repeat and leave the others plain. Don't be tempted by large pattern repeats, which will do their best to shrink your room.

If a long slim room were a person, it would attract admiring glances and look good in anything. But a spare bedroom or a family bathroom on the straight and narrow is nowhere near as desirable.

While there are many things you can do to disguise a narrow space, you need to be realistic about the room's capacity. Hallways,

broadening your outlook

for example, work hard as the home's main thoroughfare, and give an important first impression to visitors. On top of this, many of us use this area as a dumping ground for coats, shoes, work and school bags, keys and mail. Similarly, a skinny, hard-working kitchen can often find itself hoarding crockery and table linens that could easily be housed elsewhere. As a first step to your room revival, weed out items that could be stored somewhere else, and consider how much storage you'll need to keep the remainder under control.

Positioning furniture in a narrow room can be a real challenge. In a perfectly proportioned living room, a pair of sofas placed at right angles to each other looks inviting, but the effect can be bulky and cramped in a narrow space (if you can actually fit them in that way at all). Skinny bedrooms that leave no room for side tables or storage and overstretched galley kitchens are common dilemmas.

Fight the urge to 'tone down' a narrow space in order to avoid unwanted scrutiny. Consider lining up furniture or fittings if your room is too narrow for a more traditional arrangement. Similarly, experiment with small clusters of seating in a narrow sitting room, rather than attempting to squeeze everything together.

Narrow spaces can all too easily make us feel as though the walls are closing in on us. While you cannot actually alter physical width, there are many decorating tricks that will give the illusion of a wider room. Using pale, receding colours on the longest walls or creating a strong visual focal point in the room, for example, will go a long way to broadening the room's appearance.

Space saving often calls for a bit of lateral thinking. For example, leaving doors open allows a room visually to 'borrow' space from adjoining rooms and achieve a feeling of airy circulation and space. This works especially well in poorly lit areas such as hallways, as you will often gain extra natural light to boot.

golden rules
FOR NARROW SPACES

○ **keep doors open**
Prop open doors with stones, paperweights or pretty fabric bags filled with pebbles. Position furniture in next-door rooms so that it offers an enticing view from the narrow space.

○ **be bold**
Distract attention from a room's narrowness by adding a dramatic colour or painting to one of the shorter walls. If you choose a naturally advancing colour such as red or orange, it will square up the room by making the longer walls appear shorter.

○ **get horizontal**
Invest in wallpaper with horizontal stripes – or achieve the same effect with a paintbrush and a roll of masking tape. Alternatively, position a sofa or daybed with a striped loose cover at one end of the room and pile it high with striped cushions and throws.

○ pare down furniture

Think radically. One tactic is to plump for a single really generous and comfortable sofa, and add squishy cushions to dining chairs whenever extra seating is needed.

○ choose helpful flooring

Make the space appear wider by laying wooden floorboards or subtly striped carpeting crosswise. Choose a single neutral colour for your floor covering rather than a bright shade or a fussy, distracting pattern.

○ control clutter

Sort everything in the room into categories and store each type of object or set of papers in a separate file or basket. Place any item you can do without in a box. Put the box in a cupboard or garage. If you haven't retrieved it within six months, take it to a charity shop or car-boot sale.

1 A vibrant orange partition wall at one end of a child's bedroom draws the eye towards it, visually shortening the room while adding a playful note.

solutions
FOR NARROW SPACES

2 Hard-working filing trays such as these wall-mounted pockets will house the piles of papers that multiply while your back is turned. If you manage to keep on top of everyday clutter, you won't feel as though the room is closing in on you.

3 An uncluttered route through high-traffic areas is essential, so if you need to store coats in your hallway, avoid lining the longer walls with peg rails and umbrella stands. Here, a redundant corner has been utilized, and outdoor gear sits on hooks that have been added to eye-catching pieces of driftwood.

4   The dado rail has been removed from this bedroom since it was not an original feature and accentuated the narrowness of the space by 'cutting the walls in half'. The result is a clean, streamlined look that lets the eye focus on the carefully chosen decorative elements in the room.

5   A generous cushion-filled sofa fits snugly across the width of a narrow room, creating a cosy focal point. If it had been placed against one of the longer walls, the room would appear even skinnier.

6   Narrow spaces often suffer from patchy light. Here, halogen spot lighting in a hallway ceiling removes shadows and provides an even, ambient light. A dimmer switch makes it possible to ensure that this is neither harsh nor gloomy. Carefully positioned lamps in the sitting room beyond provide light for reading, while adding pools of light to attract the eye away from the entrance hall's imperfect proportions.

7   If a short wall in your narrow room has a doorway, paint both the door and surround the same colour as the wall. When the door is closed, the uniform hue will 'hide' the doorway, maximizing the wall's proportions. Use the same trick to disguise radiators.

8   Two nesting tables are worth far more than one placed in the middle of the room. If you opt for double-value furniture, there will be fewer pieces to clutter up the room. Similarly, keep occasional chairs tucked into an alcove and pull them into the centre of the room when needed.

6

7

8

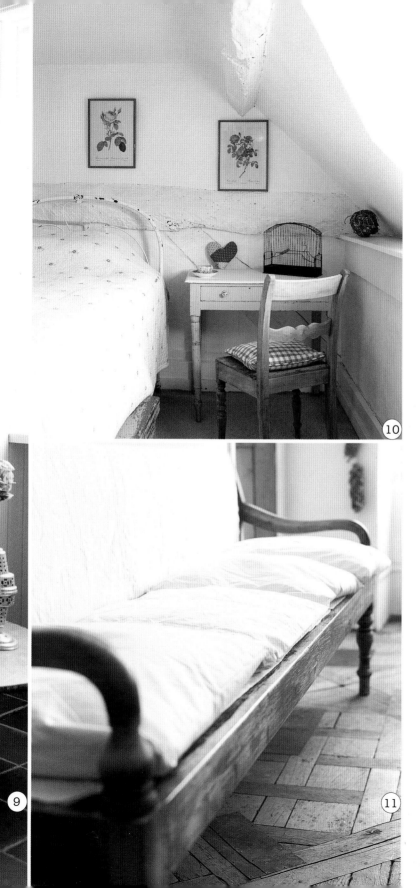

9 Candy-striped bolsters, scatter cushions and throws cover a day bed in this cosy living room. The fabrics emphasize the horizontal, stretching out the short wall against which the sofa has been placed.

10 In this tiny, low-ceilinged guest room, a pine desk doubles as a bedside and dressing table. Whitewashed walls emphasize the room's rustic charm and prevent the space from feeling claustrophobic or tunnel-like.

11 A long, narrow bench takes pride of place in a hallway, complementing the gangly proportions of the space. It offers a comfortable and stylish spot to take off outdoor shoes and relax.

12 Really strange room shapes should be celebrated. Here, a long, low sofa draws attention to the elegantly lean dimensions of the space, while a vintage swivel chair shows off the room's sensual curve.

13 An ornate mirror lends opulence to an otherwise neutral sitting room. There's no need for narrow spaces to be shy and retiring, but they work best if you stick to just one extravagant piece and tone down the other elements in the room.

14 Bathroom storage is something many of us overlook. This tall cabinet offers an abundance of hiding spaces for towels and toiletries but occupies minimal floor space.

15 Slim kitchens pose a problem if you want them to double as eating areas. The trick is to line up kitchen units that blend with your wall colour on one side of the room, reserving the other for the dining area.

16 The fixtures in this bathroom have been carefully positioned in a row, making ingenious use of what was once a redundant passageway.

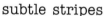

subtle stripes

Stripes in any combination stretch out narrow rooms, but timeless blue and white has a particular appeal. Paint horizontal stripes on short walls, or get a similar effect by placing a striped rug across the space or adding ticking and cushions to a sofa. The result will be a fresh, clean look that maximizes the room's width while conjuring up rustic French farmhouses, willow-patterned plates and English Cornishware.

decorating palettes
FOR NARROW SPACES

advancing effect

Give narrow rooms a focal point by painting one shorter wall in a rich, strong colour. Bold shades of red, orange, brown and yellow have an advancing effect, which squares up the space. These colours also bring character and warmth to the room while making up for its skinny shape. Mix this single block of colour with warm, neutral tones of pale string, heavy cream or soft grey.

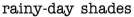

rainy-day shades

Narrow rooms may be subjected to both full sun and shade, so choose a palette that looks good in different lights. Colours made up of several shades tend to work better here than pure hues, which can appear sullied in some lights. Pale muddy tones also recede more than their clearer cousins, so they are excellent for making cramped spaces feel more spacious. Try tinting your room with warm grey, blue-grey or pinky lilac.

whitewash

If you want to give a narrow room a bright, spacious feel, there is nothing more effective than lashings of fresh white – be it in the form of paint, fabric or kitchen units. White reflects large amounts of light into interiors, appearing almost to eradicate corners and edges as it bounces from wall to wall. The result is an airy, tranquil and timeless room. Decorating any space purely in white may seem unadventurous at first, but white makes a perfect blank canvas against which to display treasured objects and artworks, and provides a powerful antidote to busy, stressful lives.

As this book shows, rooms come in all shapes and sizes. We are constantly editing and extending our homes, converting garages and removing partition walls. Older houses have evolved to accommodate the arrival of bathrooms, central heating and many other changes in the way we live. It is little wonder that we are sometimes left

changing shape

with one or two strangely proportioned spaces that defy decoration. Perhaps you have to pass through a tunnel-like passageway to enter a bedroom or have a room with several mismatching windows all set at different heights? Perhaps you are in a quandary about what to do with a disconnected L-shaped sitting area.

It is not only awkward floor plans that cause trouble. Attempting to decorate around the sloping ceilings and uneven floors that are commonplace in older houses can be an infuriating business. Country cottages of a certain age are charming until you try to paper over their lumpy, irregular walls – it is often difficult to find a single right angle to work with. Yet, despite the challenges they pose, it is the very quirkiness of these rooms that should be celebrated. The problems they present can be worked around and resolved – with some wonderfully individual results.

Choosing the right furniture and placing it correctly is important to the success of an irregularly shaped room. If you can, make life-size newspaper templates of your furniture and experiment with layouts. (Alternatively, draw the room to scale and make scaled-down templates.) You should be able to walk around each piece comfortably without bumping your head on a sloping ceiling or squeezing past a wardrobe. Consider adding small-scale furniture to the mix. A pair of tiny tray tables and a slipper chair may be able to go where no regularly sized pieces can follow. If there isn't enough room to move around freely, look at foldable, stowable and stackable furniture options and invest in custom-made storage.

Above all, don't be timid about decorating an oddly shaped room – a half-hearted attempt can make the whole thing look like a mistake. Light the room imaginatively, choose a soft colour or subtle print that you love, and use it liberally. Fill the room with special objects personal to you and enjoy the eccentricity of the space.

○ set new standards

Non-standard bathroom fixtures make sense in awkwardly shaped bathrooms. Sunken baths that are entered from one end work really well under sloping ceilings and squeezed into narrow spaces.

○ personalize storage

Have cupboards and wardrobes built to fit your space. They will look far neater than off-the-shelf storage. Also, a strategically placed floor-to-ceiling unit can be used to conceal a strange wall angle.

○ use uniform colour

Soften angles and strong lines by painting walls and ceiling either white or a pale receding colour. Camouflage radiators, skirting boards and doors in the same way. If the entrance is narrow or dark, paint the area in a lighter version of the shade used in the rest of the room to open up the space and prevent a tunnel effect.

○ cover up

If your walls are imperfect, cover them with wallpaper. Most small repeat patterns work well, but avoid geometrics, which only highlight lumps and bumps. If your walls are in good condition, wallpapers with horizontal lines can disguise sharp angles.

golden rules
FOR MISSHAPEN SPACES

○ create symmetry

The jaunty angles and unexpected layouts of irregularly shaped rooms can leave you feeling a little at sea. Counteract this by creating symmetrical displays on shelves, mantelpieces and bedside tables.

○ follow the floor

Many older homes have sloping floors or ceilings. To avoid feeling off-balance every time you enter the room, fit picture rails, dado rails and curtain tracks parallel to the floor. Disguise irregularities at ceiling height by painting the area above the picture rail in a pale receding colour. If there is a noticeable slant above curtain headings, a deep pelmet fitted close to the ceiling will conceal it.

solutions
FOR MISSHAPEN SPACES

1 In a sea of irregular angles and surfaces, a large custom-made wardrobe placed in the centre of the room creates an island of calm. The clever solution – bedhead, storage space and display area all rolled into one – offers a strong focal point.

2 Wall-to-wall neutral flooring gives cohesion to a country-style sitting room. (Avoid rugs and runners, which accentuate irregular angles.) You can unify windows of different heights with simple blinds. Mount each blind at the same level, and lower the fabric to below the top of the shortest window so that all the windows appear to be of equal height.

3 A shapely refrigerator chills out in the middle of an open-plan sitting and dining area. If a room's shape dictates that a large practical item must be in full view, invest in a handsome piece and set it against a wall painted in the same colour.

4 A skinny alcove is exactly the right width to accommodate a collection of paperback books. Unconventional nooks and crannies can do much to enhance the character of a home and should be exploited wherever possible.

5 Custom-built storage is shoe-horned into the walls of a room that also accommodates the home's main stairwell. Painted the same neutral shade as the ceiling and walls, the handle-free cupboards blend in almost seamlessly with their surroundings.

6 Non-standard fixtures can solve the puzzle of awkwardly shaped rooms, and need not be very expensive. Here, a slightly shorter than average bath fits neatly into an alcove. Distressed mirror tiles bathe the space in reflected light and give the room an air of glamour.

1

4

7 Irregular angles needn't always be disguised, and in this space they are openly celebrated. The simple right angles in the compact kitchen area draw attention to the room's unusual shape and dramatic proportions, while an absence of clutter gives the eye a clear view.

8 The awkward shape of this bedroom made finding a good position for the bed something of a challenge. The solution was to build a waist-high storage unit to act as a bedhead. The warm shade of the wall matches the wooden unit, helping to smooth out harsh angles even further.

9 A neat sofa and a low sideboard have been tucked under the eaves of this sitting room to allow easy access to the bathroom beyond. An essentially neutral scheme has been subtly brightened with splashes of blue to create a space that is cosy but far from claustrophobic.

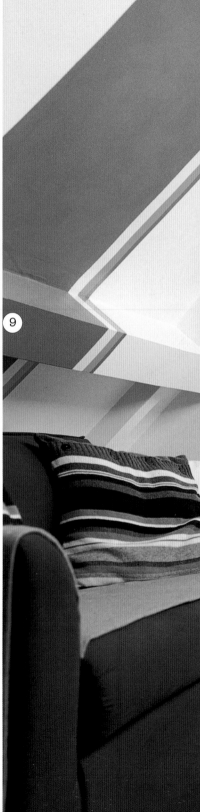

decorating palettes
FOR MISSHAPEN SPACES

ground control

Oddly shaped rooms can feel unnerving, but you can offset this effect with grounding colours. Pale tints of green, blue and grey are all naturally calming; earthy-toned neutrals are steadying; and brown used in small amounts introduces stability and warmth. Above all, trust your instincts. Choose a colour you love and paint the entire room with it to avoid the strong lines and sharp angles of wayward walls and ceilings.

gently does it

Rooms with irregular angles, particularly those with sloping ceilings, need gentle handling to avoid the impression that the walls are closing in. White schemes combined with accessories in delicate patterns and feminine tints create the right mixture of airiness and interest. For a comfortable, lived-in look, combine several designs along with a variety of personal objects.

cover up

Many wallpapers provide good camouflage for irregular walls and can make a real style statement at the same time. (But avoid geometric designs, which highlight imperfections.) If the line where the wall and ceiling meet is wobbly, choose a paper with a pale background, and use this shade for the ceiling. Designs with horizontal lines can soften sharp wall angles and visually stretch out narrow walls, giving the illusion of better proportions.

Many problem spaces can be tackled by physical alterations, but if you have lower than average ceilings you are usually stuck with them. You can bring light into a dark room by enlarging existing windows or knock two narrow spaces into one glorious square. Tiny rooms can be extended and dated ones given a fresh

aiming high

look – but, unless you pull down the entire house and start again from scratch, the roof's the limit for vertically challenged rooms.

Vogues in interior design and decoration change almost as often as the contents of our wardrobes, and not very long ago low ceilings were seen as an asset. By the middle of the 20th century, women in the developed world were voicing their disenchantment with time-consuming housework and their desire for brand-new homes that were easy to maintain. Fashionable fixtures and fittings were very plain in style, and lower ceilings promised low heating costs along with a modern, unstuffy look. At the time, people living in Victorian homes often inserted false ceilings to conceal intricate cornicing and decorated them with polystyrene ceiling tiles, which have since fallen dramatically out of favour. Cast-iron fireplaces were replaced, and outmoded door mouldings were boarded over or removed. Whatever the age of your home, it is worth tapping gently on the ceilings. You may be one of the lucky ones who simply have to remove a bit of plaster or tiling to gain extra height.

If there is no way up, console yourself with the thought that low ceilings do have some plus points. Apart from lower heating bills, you may actually prefer the cosy feeling afforded by shallow rooms. As houseboats, traditional beach huts and country cottages all prove, low ceilings can add character and charm – if you are fortunate enough to live in a cottage with exposed beams, you will probably want to make them a prominent feature of the place.

A low ceiling can also create an enclosing and comforting feeling. If the ceiling in question is in a child's bedroom, you may choose to ignore the 'heightening' suggestions in this chapter altogether and paint the ceiling a deep colour to advance and 'lower' it further. What could be lovelier for a child at night than gazing at a dreamy midnight-blue sky sprinkled with thousands of tiny silver stars?

golden rules
FOR A TALL EFFECT

○ lighten upwards

Use uplighters to direct soft light towards the ceiling, making it appear further away. They are available as freestanding pieces that can add a decorative element to the room or as unobtrusive, wall-mounted designs.

○ drop the dado

Fix a dado rail a little lower than normal (the usual height is about a third of the way up a wall) or remove it altogether. Consider replacing other elements that give away a room's scale, such as traditional fireplaces or standard-height radiators.

○ add vertical stripes

Accentuate the vertical with floor-to-ceiling stripes. Use brightly striped or tone-on-tone wallpaper, or achieve the same effect by painting the room with alternate bands of complementary colours – but make sure you use a plumb line to avoid wobbly stripes.

○ paint ceilings white

Opt for white paint with a sheen finish that will bounce even more light into the room than a matt white product. Match the wall area above picture rails to the ceiling colour rather than to the rest of the walls. Lengthen walls without picture rails by painting from the floor (including skirting boards) to the top of the coving in the same shade.

○ shorten skirting

Replace an existing skirting board with a simple shallow design or remove it altogether. Paint boards the same colour as the walls; the room will look shallower if they match the floor.

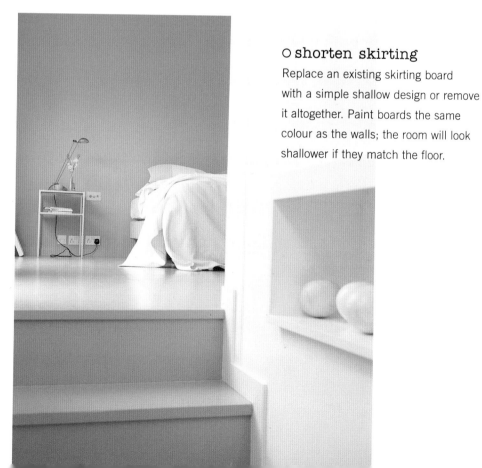

○ lengthen curtains

Treat windows to full-length curtains regardless of their size to stress the longer lines and draw attention to the windows and the views beyond them. If floor-length drapes are unsuitable, blend in shorter curtains by keeping them the same colour as the walls.

1 A laid-back day bed looks comfortable and inviting in its neutral surroundings. The clever placing of organic sprigs and branches on the shelves and around the fireplace enhances the sense of height in this sitting room.

2 A collection of found objects adorns a vintage plan chest. Interesting displays at dado level or below distract attention from the lack of ceiling height. The spindly wood carvings and elegant orchid in this group further emphasize the vertical.

solutions FOR A TALL EFFECT

3 The pleasing view of a patio garden draws the eye away from the size and height of the galley kitchen. Consider enlarging the openings for windows and doors to give better views either through your home or to the exterior.

4 Floor-to-ceiling cupboards in the dressing area of a bedroom offer discreet storage that is less jarring on the eye than freestanding pieces would be. Sleek, narrow cupboards and skinny door handles both emphasize the vertical. A long, low day bed enhances the illusion of height.

5

5 The exposed beams of a converted 18th-century mill add character and warmth; but the beams have been kept pale and the walls painted a chalky white to give a feeling of airiness and space to an essentially low and restricted room.

6 A teetering chest of drawers is taken down a peg or two with a lick of white paint. Tall pieces of furniture attract attention to low ceilings, so camouflage them with a shade that matches your wall colour. This technique will also make your room look larger.

7 Uplighters and neat halogen spots illuminate ceilings, increasing the perception of height. Avoid low-hanging pendant lights and eye-catching chandeliers in shallow spaces – no matter how gorgeous they are, they will only draw attention to the room's imperfections.

8 A chunky granite kerbstone makes an unusual and tactile step into a spare bedroom. The eye-catching slab effectively distracts attention from the restricted ceiling height beyond.

shock tactics

Splashes of bright colour or pattern at eye level or lower keep the eye moving from side to side rather than looking upwards and taking in the proportions of a shallow room. Keep the overall scheme neutral, then add accessories in the form of cushions, throws and keepsakes. Objects linked by design or colour, set at intervals around a room, will give a balance and rhythm to the space.

decorating palettes
FOR A TALL EFFECT

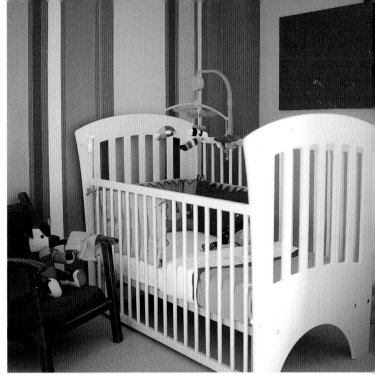

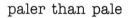

paler than pale

White provides a cleansing, space-enhancing backdrop against which to display possessions, while its reflective qualities maximize daylight. Brilliant white contains blue pigments and can look stark and cold, so choose a chalky or pale neutral tone. Use white to blur the dimensions of a shallow room by painting the ceiling and walls in the same tone. If you need colour, a pale receding tint such as sky-blue or shell-pink would also be effective used in this way.

up and away

Tall stripes draw the eye upwards, giving an illusion of extra height. Add fun to a child's room with bold vertical stripes of varying widths painted in cheerful colours. Choose a subtler statement for grown-up spaces, such as curtains with skinny, elegant stripes or neutral tongue-and-groove boarding. Slimline bookcases, grandfather clocks and standard lamps all accentuate a vertical scheme beautifully.

Just as plants turn their leaves to face the nearest window, humans crave natural light. Sunshine offers a feel-good factor that is hard to beat, so it's no wonder that many of us dream of escaping for whole summers to Italian villas or French farmhouses. While builders of modern homes are increasingly addressing our desire for plentiful

lightening up

light, this has not always been a priority. The Victorians did their best to screen furnishings and pictures (along with their pale skins) from the sun, as much of their housing stock shows. Without plenty of natural light, even tall, spacious rooms can feel gloomy and airless.

Don't despair if your home isn't filled with sun-drenched spaces; you may not need as much light as you think in every room. Reserve the sunniest spots for daytime places such as breakfast rooms and sitting rooms. In rooms where light is at a premium, consider the activities you enjoy there. Place a favourite reading chair or sewing table near the main light source, and relegate the television and bookcases to shadier corners.

Remember, too, that there are advantages to dark rooms. In spaces that receive little or no direct sunlight, there is no chance of sun damage, so treat yourself to beautiful furnishing fabrics and display treasured photographs and artwork there. Dark rooms make good bedrooms. Waking up to bright light can feel uncomfortable, especially if you are not a morning person. A dim dining area can become an enchanting evening retreat when painted in rich colours and bathed in candlelight. Dark rooms can be intimate and cosseting, so dress them in pools of warm, sculptural light and celebrate their moodiness.

Apart from the imaginative use of glass and reflective surfaces, the element that can do most to brighten a space is the removal or modification of a partition wall. Removing walls will make your home much lighter – but not everyone feels comfortable living in a completely open-plan space. One solution is to replace them with movable screens, chest-height walls or curtains hooked onto a ceiling-mounted track. Alternatively, consider installing partition walls made with glass bricks or sections of frosted glass that allow light to flood through. If you can, enlarge existing windows or turn them into French windows to create a lighter space with a broader outlook.

○ uncover windows

Don't waste light by obscuring windows with curtain edges and blinds. Fit extended poles that allow drapes to be swept back onto the wall. Set brackets higher than usual so that blinds can be drawn clear. Opt for traditional shutters that fold out of the way during the day. Banish gathered net curtains or swap them for half-height, sheer flat panels.

golden rules
FOR ENHANCING LIGHT

○ add artificial

Boost low levels of daylight with artificial lighting. Avoid traditional, centrally placed ceiling fittings because they are unflattering and will leave corners in shadow. Halogen spots offer natural-looking white light. Combine them with tungsten bulbs fitted into table and standard lamps to give pools of warm inviting light.

○ be flexible

Consider ways of accessing light without losing privacy. For example, chest-height walls share light between two defined spaces. Movable screens can add a decorative quality. Floor-to-ceiling sliding doors look solid when closed but can be opened to allow light to flood in.

○ shine on

Adopt a magpie's instinct for sparkly and shiny surfaces. Mirrors and glossy finishes bounce light around a room, making it appear larger and brighter. Choose kitchen units and appliances in gleaming stainless steel. Enrich dining rooms with sparkling glassware, and treat bathrooms to jazzy mirrored splashbacks.

○ let light in

Look outdoors to make the most of every scrap of light. Plants and shrubs may appear attractive trailing over windows, but they are depleting your light supply, so prune them back. Paint garden fences and walls white or a very pale colour to bounce light into the interior. Lay pale-coloured paving stones below doors and windows for a lightening effect.

○ get more glass

Add skylights or partition walls made with glass bricks or frosted glass wherever your home's layout will allow. If you are unable to make more ambitious changes, simply inserting glass panels into internal doors will make a big difference.

solutions
FOR ENHANCING LIGHT

1 A low ceiling and small windows made this sitting area feel dark and uninspiring. The owners removed part of the ceiling and transformed the room into a double-height, light-filled space. White walls and sofas and a polished floor all reflect light.

2 This hallway would have been dark and airless – but, by leaving the kitchen above open on two sides, the whole space is filled with light.

3 The unusual layout of this home has advantages other than shared light. The kitchen is the hub of the home, and a welcoming atmosphere pervades the house upon entering. The owners love to smell coffee brewing as they walk upstairs.

4   This kitchen's open-plan layout takes advantage of natural light in the adjoining dining and sitting areas. A large overhead lighting panel provides character and effective illumination.

5   A table lamp placed on the floor provides warm tungsten light that has a sculptural quality while illuminating a corner of the room that may otherwise have appeared dingy.

6   Lavish gloomy rooms with lots of inexpensive household candles and enjoy their flickering glow.

7   Frosted-glass panels mounted into sliding doors provide an elegant solution to a shady hallway. Large mirrored panels and a glass coffee table magnify the available light.

8   The wide doorway and internal window in this apartment allow the dining area to borrow light from the living room, while polished wooden floors and pale walls reflect available light.

9   Along with the white walls outside, glossy white panels above large French windows magnify the available light in this bedroom.

10   Sliding glass doors occupy a whole wall in this minimalist room, allowing the maximum amount of light to flood into the space. Whitewashed garden walls bounce light into the room.

4

5

6

11 Glass roofs offer additional light and sky views. Consider installing blinds in rooms that receive direct sunlight to avoid a baking greenhouse effect on hot sunny days.

12 The tiny kitchen at the back of this apartment relies on the adjoining sitting area for daylight. Fluorescent strips behind frosted-glass panels illuminate the area and cleverly give the illusion of a window.

13 While gloomy living spaces may dampen your spirits, dimly lit entrance areas can be positively dangerous. Unlike wall or ceiling lights that may dazzle as you climb the stairs, floor-level halogen spots provide excellent illumination while giving the treads a sculptural quality.

14 Skylights offer a perfect solution for bathrooms, flooding light into the room while allowing privacy to be maintained. Here, large openings in the ceiling give a minimalist bathroom a calming ethereal quality.

unrepentantly rich

If you can afford to set aside a room for use only in the evenings, you can ignore all the rules about lightening and brightening. Celebrate after-hours with a rich, saturated colour palette. Dining rooms look fabulous in deep red, which also enhances the appetite. A purple bedroom is decadent, while a deep-orange sitting area will encourage animated discussion. Embellish your scheme with tactile furnishings and glittering accessories to create a feast for the senses.

decorating palettes
FOR ENHANCING LIGHT

upon reflection

Pale tints contain large quantities of light-reflecting white, making them perfect for decorating rooms that are on the dark side. You can have too much of a good thing, however, and a purely white or cream scheme may sometimes appear stark and clinical, particularly in artificial light. A simple way to add warmth to a barely-there base of rich cream or palest blue is to choose furnishings and accessories that introduce accents of golden brown, earthy orange or shades of plum.

warm and inviting

The natural light that penetrates into north-facing
rooms is beautifully diffused and very even, but it
tends to be on the cold side. You can counteract
this by using warm colours to help compensate
for the absence of direct sunlight. Choose lively
shades of orange, russet and sunny yellow that will
cheer up your space. Use these advancing shades
carefully if your room is small. Paler versions of
the same colours will give a similar effect without
appearing to reduce a room's proportions.

Although we may not like to admit it, most of us are voyeurs at heart. Who can resist gazing through a lit window or peeking through a half-open door? The trouble is, we all may love to look, but few of us want to be spied on in our private moments. Home is a sanctuary, a place where we can, if we want, wear sloppy unflattering clothes,

creating privacy

practise those disco moves and stop trying to hold in our stomach muscles. To counteract the stresses of busy working lives, home needs to be a place where we can relax unobserved.

All humans love to feel cosy and secure when relaxing or sleeping. For centuries, four-poster beds provided protection from draughty interiors and privacy from others, since whole families often slept in the same room. Today, many of us aspire to master bedrooms with oodles of space – and then find them just too big. Open-plan living spaces work brilliantly for entertaining and family activities but they can sometimes make us feel a little lost. Dividing rooms into manageable zones with screens, curtains and dividing doors can make large living areas feel more comfortable. For people with home-based employment, a screened office area provides the privacy to work and also the freedom to leave out materials when you choose.

Millions of us live cheek-by-jowl with our neighbours in densely populated areas, so it is not surprising that we guard our personal spaces fiercely. However, while privacy is important, it would be a mistake to exclude the outside world entirely.

The following pages offer many screening ideas. When deciding how to dress your windows it is important to opt for coverage that allows plenty of sunlight into the room – but that should not be the only criterion. The materials you choose should feel at home with the rest of the room. Choose simple, flat linen panels or clean-lined Perspex shutters to complement a contemporary minimalist interior. Add metres of floaty sheer fabrics or lace panels to soften windows in a feminine or romantic room, or an intricately decorated folding screen to provide a bohemian or ethnically inspired space with interest and texture. Above all, view the problem of creating privacy as a welcome challenge. A beautifully dressed window offers an enticing view of the world.

○ use less not more

Keep window dressings to a minimum to maximize natural light and make the most of views. Café curtains or half-height shutters look charming and are suitable for many situations. If you need to screen the whole window, choose sheer flat panels instead of gathered curtains.

golden rules
FOR GREATER PRIVACY

○ dress to suit

Choose a window dressing that works well with the rest of the room. A frilly café curtain would look out of place in a minimal setting, and frosted-glass panels would not suit a country home.

○ cocoon yourself

Cover your bed with a canopy, curtains or metres of frothy netting. Make cavernous spaces cosier by placing open shelves or a sofa across the room.

○ go green

Window boxes and potted plants make excellent natural screens and can do much to improve an imperfect view. Choose flowers for colour, herbs for aroma, or both. Alternate arrangements throughout the year to ensure good coverage.

○ mould your space

If your home isn't big enough to accommodate both private spaces for sleeping and working and large communal areas for entertaining, introduce folding screens, ceiling-mounted curtain tracks or sliding doors to create a flexible space that can adapt to suit your needs.

○ think high and low

Consider raising windows or installing skylights – you'll gain unadulterated sky views and more daylight. Look also at lowering your horizons. A sunken bath, for example, allows the bather to sit in it without being spied on from outside.

1 Strip curtains are fun, generally inexpensive and provide privacy without blocking out too much light. Designs vary greatly, from candy-coloured beaded shapes to transparent shells or tiny mirrored balls. Here, a sophisticated monochrome chain-mail curtain screens a bedroom from the main living area.

solutions
FOR GREATER PRIVACY

2 Replace the lower panes of your windows with frosted glass for a cool, minimalist look. If you are not sure whether to take the plunge, place tracing paper over the window to try out the effect.

3 A plain white roller-blind fitted 'upside down' allows coverage of either the whole window or only the lower half.

4 A funky Perspex screen looks at home in a hip New York apartment. Privacy is maintained, and the soft yellow-orange light that is filtered into the room is an added bonus.

5 Frosted panels, which can look stark in some settings, are softened by a pair of patterned sheer fabric panels that give the room a strong style statement.

6 A shoulder-height wall delineates a sleeping area in an open-plan home. The partition also provides a headboard and a place to install bedside lighting.

7 The beds of two siblings have been placed at right angles to offer the children some breathing space as they sleep.

8 Panels or curtains made of sheer white cotton or linen offer classic inexpensive window coverage. The look is softer than blinds or shutters.

9 Sliding glass doors allow light to be shared between a bedroom and an en-suite bathroom. The frosted panels mean that privacy can be enjoyed by both sleepers and bathers.

10 Once found only in schools or offices, venetian blinds offer sleek, directional coverage. They can also let in fresh air while keeping out bright sun and the glances of passers-by.

contemporary

Clean-lined modernity is achieved by combining minimal styling with contemporary materials. Dress windows simply, adding frosted-glass panels where needed, or do a modern take on traditional shutters, using Perspex instead of wood. Stiffened sheer fabric blinds give a sharper look than curtains.

decorating palettes
FOR GREATER PRIVACY

classic

For a timeless look, choose sturdy materials and classic design. Easy-to-use wooden shutters offer complete privacy and also prevent interiors from overheating on sunny days. Although their slats allow in some light, half-height versions are good for screening windows simply from passers-by. Flat linen panels add softness while retaining a clean, fresh look. Versatile Venetian blinds cover the whole window, but can be angled as desired to maximize light or privacy.

romantic

Metres of sheer, floaty fabrics add charm and femininity to windows. Soften hard edges with gathered white curtains, gauzy nets or even lengths of cheap sari fabric. Search out pieces of antique lace or beaded fabrics that will glisten in sunlight and add romance to your interior.

If you have a bland room on your hands, the chances are it's your own fault. Ask yourself a few questions. Does browsing through paint charts send you into a panic of indecision that results in a bulk purchase of magnolia emulsion? Do you choose furniture expressly because it is plain and unlikely to attract attention? Do you buy

adding character

accessories you don't love, just because they'll 'go with everything'? Don't despair if this sounds familiar. You are certainly not the only one who is guilty of off-white overload – and it's relatively easy to inject some life into lacklustre rooms.

Good taste does not have to be boring, but it is hardly surprising that so many of us play it safe. Decorating and furniture purchases can be very expensive, and you will probably be living with your decisions for quite a while. Nobody wants to be left with a dated sofa a couple of years down the line.

Recent fashions are also partly to blame. The trend in the 1990s was for minimalist interiors that were super-slick, predominantly white and fairly expressionless. Happily, this is now being replaced by a more relaxed, 'anything goes' approach that leaves plenty of room to include mismatched belongings and to inject personal style.

The trick to creating an interesting room is to buy classic, neutral big-ticket items, and have some fun with wall colour and accessories that can be changed inexpensively. Choose the colours, patterns, fabrics and textures that you love, and display keepsakes that mean something to you. Keeping a scrapbook of the styles you admire will reward you with visual inspiration when you are ready to decorate. This will make it easier to experiment, rather than reaching for the same neutral shades and characterless accessories. Fill the pages with paint colour cards, fabric and wallpaper swatches, postcards and pages of interiors torn from magazines. Choosing a wall shade can be particularly daunting. If you are nervous about using colour, buy several test pots, and try out each one on a large piece of card. Study the cards at different times of the day before you choose a winner.

Whatever your style, this chapter will give you confidence to put your own mark on a room, so have fun and let the flavour permeate. After all, if you can't be yourself at home, where can you?

golden rules

FOR EXTRA INTEREST

○ **make a statement**

Search for a single show-
stopping piece to provide a
focal point. A large, lavishly
gilded mirror, an ornately
carved bed or a wildly
oversized print could be all
that an uninteresting room
needs to regain a feeling
of fun and personality.

○ **mix and match**

Blend ethnic with contemporary
pieces, streamlined with ornate
objects, and mass-produced
with one-of-a-kind finds. Add
a smattering of various patterns.
Don't worry about overdoing it.
Just build up layers gradually,
so you'll know when to stop.

○ **be bold**

Attack bland interiors with strong,
saturated colour, even if you paint
just one wall or a chimney breast.
Alternatively, inject interest with
an eye-catching accent shade.
Add splashes of burnt orange
to a pale blue room, or lime and
mossy greens to a cream palette.

○ introduce texture

Decorate with a variety of textures and materials to create a tactile interior. A mixture of old and new, rough and smooth, or shiny and matt will keep you entertained and stimulated.

○ use wallpaper

Brighten up a dull space and create instant atmosphere with a cheerful wallpaper design. (Wallpaper will also help to hide any imperfections in the walls.)

○ show your style

Fill the room with objects that mean something to you and resist the urge to buy tasteful ornaments that match your décor. Interiors need soul to be inviting, so it's essential that you show what you are made of. Rotate your displays frequently to keep the room fresh.

1 The neutral scheme in this sitting room has been given an injection of colour by the addition of a single striking painting. The bold orange and rich green in the artwork are echoed in the sumptuous velvet cushions, which add texture to the room.

solutions
FOR EXTRA INTEREST

2 Bold colour can be very striking when used sparingly. Minimal decoration is necessary in this nursery, where an electric-blue wall is a perfect backdrop for a simple paper shade.

3 It's hard to create a stylish home office when you have a great deal of paperwork to deal with. Here, a handful of red boxes provides both order and visual interest in a potentially dreary desk area.

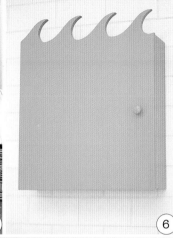

5

6

7

8

4 Plain white bathrooms may be a safe, sensible option, but imagine how cheerful a morning shower would feel if you were surrounded by zingy yellow tiles.

5 When adding interest and personal style to a room, anything goes. Here, a favourite pair of party shoes and a skinny high-backed chair introduce fun and quirkiness to a work station.

6 Curvaceous and unusual shapes enhance visual interest. This plain white bathroom is pepped up by a bright, wave-topped cabinet.

7 White walls make rooms look larger and lighter, and they need not be boring as long as you accessorize them well. This room is given vitality by a line-up of pretty dresses, together with colourful pegged-up keepsakes.

8 Antiques needn't be treated with total reverence. Here, a romantic floral print fabric livens up an imposing armoire.

9 If you are fortunate enough to have a spacious hallway, dress it like an art gallery. Treasured eye-catching objects placed in a hall will set the mood for the rest of your home.

10 Avoiding blandness needn't mean a riot of bright colours. In this elegant bedroom, a single rich accent shade is used in several tactile textures to give warmth and interest to an otherwise minimal space.

11 While a bold colour can brighten up a dull room, large amounts of a single shade can look solid and oppressive. Here, a variety of cheerful shades have been used to cover a banquette, creating a friendly playroom.

9

10

ethnic style

India provides a visual feast that
is a perfect antidote to bland rooms.
Choose from shades such as turmeric,
saffron, chilli-red and hot pink from
a flavourful colour palette inspired by
Indian spices. Mix ethnic patterns with
gold-edged sari-style fabrics to add
richness and depth to your scheme.
Keep floors and walls predominantly
neutral to avoid sensory overload, and
allow the ethnic touches to sing out.

decorating palettes
FOR EXTRA INTEREST

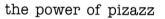

the power of pizazz

A shot or two of strong colour will transform an uninspiring room. Create a cheerful, contemporary space by painting a single chimney breast, or covering whole walls and reupholstering furniture in zingy shades. For shrinking violets, a single well-placed chair or a couple of cushions may be all you need to brighten a neutral interior. Look out for striking artwork or a colourful rug, which would give a similar uplifting effect to a dull room.

genuine originality

Ignore high-street trends and blend all kinds of furniture and accessories for a truly original look. The beauty of an eclectic style is that you needn't throw anything away just because it doesn't match everything else. In fact, the more diverse your belongings are, the better. Try mixing contemporary dining chairs with an old scrubbed pine table, or an elegant chandelier with worn leather sofas to create a room that is genuinely your own.

If your home fails to give you a warm welcome whenever you return, there is something amiss. Rooms that feel chilly are neither relaxing nor comfortable to be in, and certainly won't help you wind down properly after a hard day's work. While feeling cosy is not only about a room's physical temperature, you need to get heat levels right

warming up

before looking at decorative solutions. If the thermostat is turned up but you are still reaching for a third jumper, ask a heating engineer to advise on whether you need more radiators and whether your boiler has the capacity to cope with extra work. Consider installing double-glazing if you don't already have it. The secondary panes keep heat in effectively, and will reduce fuel bills. If you are unwilling to fit double-glazing for aesthetic or practical reasons, heavy interlined curtains will provide invaluable insulation during the evenings and will prevent heat loss overnight. Finally, small draughts may seem insignificant to you, but they can have a big impact on heat levels, so block off unused fireplaces and repair ill-fitting doors.

We all recognize a cosy, inviting room when we see it, but it can be difficult to reproduce that feel-good factor in your home. Even when the temperature is right, some rooms look downright miserable. North-facing rooms suffer from a cool light and no direct sunshine, while lofty interiors with barely dressed windows can make you feel lost and vulnerable. However, warmth is partly a state of mind, and our brains rely on visual cues along with physical sensations. Tests show that people feel several degrees warmer in a room decorated with sunny shades than in a plain white space, even when there is no actual difference in temperature. Because of this, there is much that can be done decoratively to change the mood in chilly-feeling spaces. Even simple lighting tricks can make a big difference. For example, you can create a cosier interior by placing several light sources around a room rather than resorting to a single overhead fitting.

The next time you find yourself in a cosy space, try to identify the elements that contribute to the room's success. Whether you want to create a welcoming guest room or a family den, adding elements such as rich advancing colour, sensual textures, soft light or a strong focal point will give a warm heart to the most soulless of interiors.

golden rules

FOR FEELING COSY

○ lower ceilings

Bring lofty ceilings down a peg or two by painting the area above the picture rail a warm shade that is deeper than the walls. (If you don't already have a rail, install one.) Choose pendant lights and hang them at picture-rail height or lower to create an intimate feel. Avoid uplighters, which add to the sense of height.

○ minimize contrast

Avoid a mix of only very pale or dark objects. Such schemes are jarring on the eye and can appear stark. Add mid-toned elements to offset the two extremes and give a friendlier look. For example, balance a mahogany dresser and white-painted floor with warming burnt-orange walls.

○ use cosier colours

Choose paint and fabrics in warm saturated tones of orange, red, yellow and golden brown to cheer up chilly rooms. Steer clear of very dark or matt shades, which absorb too much light and make murky rooms look even gloomier. Paint ceilings and woodwork a chalky or cream shade.

○ turn up the heat

Draw attention to heat sources. Install a working fireplace or coal-effect gas fire to add both warmth and a focal point. If a fireplace is impractical, dress ugly radiators in elegant covers and top them with eye-catching displays.

○ add comfort elements

Make sure that beds, sofas and chairs appear as comfortable and inviting as they feel. Introduce generous helpings of cushions, pillows and throws in interesting patterns and alluring textures to transform pieces of furniture into cosy nests.

○ choose warm light

Avoid halogen and fluorescent bulbs that provide neutral or cool light. Choose tungsten bulbs instead, which cast a warm yellowish glow. Use candles as an instant fix; the light they give is warm, flattering and inexpensive.

1 Guest bedrooms can often appear unlived-in and a little heartless. This twin room bucks the trend with its earthy wall colour, textured bedspreads and soft fringed blankets on the beds, worn wooden furniture and unusual artwork. A coolie lampshade casts a pool of intimate light during the evenings.

solutions
FOR FEELING COSY

2 Wall-to-wall carpet insulates interiors and feels delicious underfoot. Choose a tufted wool covering in a warm neutral shade and lay it throughout your home.

3 The sturdy rustic furniture could look austere in this minimalist dining area; however, the simple rounded shapes of the artwork and pottery, along with warming touches of burnt orange, make the space feel relaxed and welcoming.

4 As this bathroom shows, ultra-minimalist interiors need not feel unwelcoming. The rounded shapes of the sandstone bath and polished plaster walls provide a simple yet sensual sanctuary.

5 Older furniture moulded into shape over the years can be far more comfortable than pristine new pieces, so don't discard old favourites if they are still serviceable. Here, a seat cushion has been covered with plush velvet to contrast with the smooth leather of a vintage armchair.

6 Warm up interiors instantly with layers of tactile fabrics. Fold throws over armchairs, pile sofas high with plush cushions, and dress windows with rich silky curtains.

7 The choice of paint colour for functional or high-traffic areas is important, since there is often little room for soft furnishings or accessories. Here, a reddish-brown shade gives warm earthy appeal to a utilitarian kitchen.

8 If strong colour isn't your thing, choose neutral shades with warm hues. Here honey-toned walls, buff files and boxes, and a textured sisal rug give a spacious and orderly feel to a small study-cum-spare-bedroom.

natural warmth

Glorious autumnal foliage is a great source of inspiration. De-ice chilly rooms with a natural palette of golden yellow, rich brown, burnt orange and flaming red. Keep your scheme fresh with splashes of mossy green and use chalky white for ceilings. Choose medium-toned oak or pine rather than pale beech or maple for furniture and floors.

decorating palettes

FOR FEELING COSY

textural heaven

Texture can bring warmth, depth and personality to interiors, so invest in feel-good fabrics and robust floor coverings, and root out tactile keepsakes. An eclectic mix will delight the senses, so combine rough elements with smooth, shiny with matt and old with new. Place a polished brass lamp on a knobbly wooden table, for example, or pile brightly coloured silk cushions onto a neutral linen sofa.

hot and spicy

Turn up the heat with hot vibrant colours. Choose just one cheerful shade, or mix and match the brights you love, be they red and pink, or orange and emerald-green. Use pattern freely, and mingle several complementary designs. If your cold room is also small, it may be unable to cope with explosions of colour, so choose paler versions of spicy shades for the walls and add bright colour with accessories.

Is your room showing its age? Has it lost its joie de vivre? Is it no longer getting the admiring glances it used to? If so, the time has come for a freshening-up session. It is hard to pinpoint what makes a room look dated. While furniture and furnishings are often to blame, the problem cannot be solved simply by buying into the latest home

giving refreshment

trends. Have you ever given away a tired piece of furniture only to discover that it looks hip and fresh in its new home? Old-fashioned features such as fireplaces and mouldings may seem immovable, but they can often be altered or made to blend into the background. As for decorating choices, don't feel you have to sacrifice a love of floral prints or abandon a stripped-pine table for the sake of modernity. The trick is to avoid an overload of any one style or pattern and leave space around items so they can be enjoyed.

It is easy to understand why we hold onto a style for too long. Decorating can be expensive and choices need to last. Sometimes you know you are barking up the wrong tree in terms of style, but it is easy to fall into the trap of buying items that go with everything else, and then it's hard to change direction. In other words, you become stuck in a rut. Of course, if money were no obstacle, you could just throw everything out, choose fresh furnishings and decorate yourself up to date. But, while it sounds tempting to start with a clean slate, rooms always look best when they have been allowed to evolve gradually. Familiar belongings become old friends, and it is kinder to update objects than to discard them. Besides, constantly replacing old pieces with new may result in your home taking on the appearance of a high-street store.

There are clear ground rules for updating spaces. Coloured bathroom suites can be soothed with neutral flooring and walls, along with replacement taps and fittings. Full-length curtains or simple blinds tend to look better than shorter drapes. Matt chrome finishes are more fashionable than shiny brass fittings. But the main take-home points for creating longer-lasting interiors involve both restraint and attention to detail. In a nutshell, use the prints, patterns and colours you love, but take care not to use too many at once – and, yes, new door handles really would make a difference.

○ get a handle on it

Update doors and windows with replacement handles and catches. As a rule, brass and shiny finishes are yesterday's news, so opt for matt and chrome fittings. Fit new light switch plates for a cohesive contemporary look.

golden rules
FOR UPDATING SPACES

○ cover up

Camouflage anything that has had its day. Have a simple MDF cover made to fit over an exisiting fireplace without damaging it. Alternatively, paint both fireplace and surrounding wall white to minimize and freshen. (You can disguise cumbersome furniture by painting the wall a similar shade.) Re-upholster sofas and chairs in up-to-date fabrics.

○ darken wood

Paint dated furniture in solid matt shades (avoid the distressed look, which is also waning). Sand and stain pale floorboards a richer shade for an instant uplift (add a high-gloss varnish to ensure maximum daylight reflection).

○ give it space

Give potentially dated elements plenty of breathing space. Flank fireplaces and furniture with neutral walls instead of trying to hide them alongside fussy wallpaper. Adorn surfaces with a few large, modern objects, or group ornaments for a cohesive display.

○ match mouldings

Make sure mouldings and architraves reflect the era in which your house was built. Unless you live in a 1960s home, replace shallow flat skirting with boards in keeping with the building's age. Remove false mouldings from flat doors or replace the doors with salvaged originals.

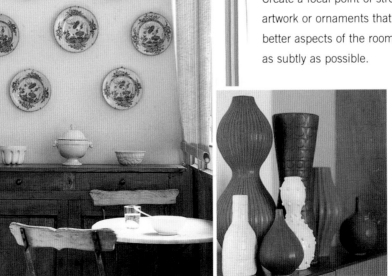

○ divert attention

Create a focal point of strong wall colour, striking artwork or ornaments that will attract the eye to the better aspects of the room. Decorate weaker areas as subtly as possible.

1 If you are stuck with a dated feature such as a 1980s-style breakfast bar, exploit it rather than disguise it. Replace hefty pine or chrome bar stools with sleek sculptural alternatives that create a deliberately retro look.

2 While retro is all the rage, an overload of one era can make a home look like a museum. By contrast, trainers stacked beneath a pair of 1950s vases give an unstuffy, lived-in feel.

solutions
FOR UPDATING SPACES

3 A pared-down room containing well-chosen objects is the essence of modernity. Where this window would once have been festooned with elaborate curtains, a simple slatted blind shows off the elegant proportions of the space. In this setting, modern and retro pieces blend beautifully.

4 Exposed brick and venetian blinds may smack of the 1980s, but a wash of chalky white paint softens and brightens the space. White furniture and shelves add charm to this child's bedroom.

5 Updating your home needn't mean throwing away treasured possessions. Here, a seemingly casual grouping of chairs and paintings looks fresh and uncluttered, thanks to a uniform palette of greens and yellow.

6 Claw-footed baths don't have to have traditional brass fittings or be set in luxurious surroundings. Giving a period piece a modern treatment makes it look bang up-to-date. Here, an enormous print and chrome taps freshen up a Victorian tub.

7 Kitchen units in bright colours or with fancy mouldings are definitely showing their age. Give cabinet doors a coat of white paint or replace them with painted MDF panels. The whitewash will also allow ageing washing machines and fridges to blend in with their surroundings.

8 Floral prints are timeless, but too many together can look stifling and dated. This airy and feminine bedroom has been created by a limited use of florals against a neutral background.

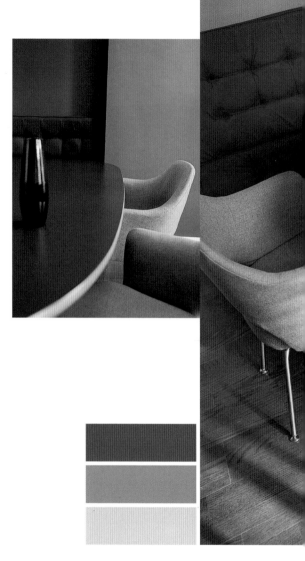

retro chic

If the fixtures and fittings in your room suggest a bygone decade, why not go with the flow? Styles of the 1950s, 1960s and 1970s are much in fashion, and searching for vintage pieces in second-hand shops and car-boot sales can be tremendous fun. Leave lots of neutral space around objects to create a retro look rather than a period recreation. Everyday modern essentials will also prevent your home taking on the feel of a museum, so don't put the sound system out of sight.

decorating palettes
FOR UPDATING SPACES

striking it rich

As we demand increasingly flexibility from our homes to accommodate both modern family life and relaxed entertaining, it's little wonder that neutral schemes are so popular. But deeper shades are currently more fashionable than the pale and uninteresting variety. Add bites of chocolate-brown and splashes of mocha to give atmosphere and depth to neutral interiors. Fill your space with indulgent textures in rich earthy tones, mixing silky with smooth, shiny with rough, and old with new.

flower power

Floral-covered fabrics and wallpapers are a perennial decorating favourite, but placing print upon print in the same room will achieve a Victoriana look that has clearly had its day. Weeding out several patterns will make a feature of the remaining designs while creating a calmer interior. Let flowers breathe by alternating them with neutral shades or solid restful colours such as soft blue or brownish pink. The resulting room will be a relaxed and feminine take on modern style.

Spaces with a single flaw are relatively easy to tackle, but if your room has more than one trouble spot you must consider the impact of two or more sets of rules when planning your attack. Even if the room has multiple flaws,

combined problems

focus on the two most awkward factors to avoid a total decorating paralysis. Whatever the mixture of imperfections, the following pages will show you how to marry together solutions. First, identify the two adjectives that most closely describe your room's problems – one from the headings across the top of the chart and the other from the column on the left of the page. Where the two columns meet on the grid, you will discover a helpful list of decorating do's and don'ts.

	small	narrow	misshapen
small		**do** pare down furniture; invest in dual-function pieces **don't** paint a striking, advancing colour on one wall **don't** light each corner of the room – this will draw attention to skinny proportions.	**do** lighten walls and ceilings with pale receding shades **do** make a central, symmetrical statement in the centre of the room **don't** use wallpaper, unless it's the tiniest of prints
narrow	**do** pare down furniture; invest in dual-function pieces **don't** paint a striking, advancing colour on one wall **don't** light each corner of the room – this will draw attention to skinny proportions		**do** use the same pale colour for walls and ceilings, but paint a single wall in an advancing shade **do** fit floor-to-ceiling cupboards across a short wall to disguise awkward angles and improve proportions **don't** worry about symmetrical arrangements
misshapen	**do** lighten walls and ceilings with pale receding shades **do** make a central, symmetrical statement in the centre of the room **don't** use wallpaper, unless it's the tiniest of prints	**do** use the same pale colour for walls and ceilings, but paint a single wall in an advancing shade **do** fit floor-to-ceiling cupboards across a short wall to disguise awkward angles and improve proportions **don't** worry about symmetrical arrangements	
low-ceilinged	**do** use uplighters to give the illusion of added height and space **do** drop dado height and shorten skirting boards **do** use full-length curtains **don't** use vertical stripes	**do** paint ceilings white or a very pale shade **do** create a strong focal point on a short wall **don't** use vertical stripes	**do** use wallpaper, but avoid designs with horizontal stripes **do** paint walls, skirting boards and ceilings the same pale shade **don't** decorate with vertical stripes
dark	**do** make use of shiny and reflective surfaces **do** soften dark furniture with pale cushions or throws **don't** use either advancing wall colours or receding shades that are very pale; opt for a middle ground that makes dark rooms warmer and less gloomy	**do** boost daylight levels with halogen bulbs **do** use reflective and sparkly surfaces **do** lay pale, neutral flooring **don't** add screens or partitions	**do** paint the area above the picture rail a pale receding colour **do** boost low daylight with various artificial lights **don't** paint the entire room a pale colour; paint one wall a richer shade
overlooked	**do** dress windows in a pared-down, simple style **don't** cover beds with a canopy or curtains **don't** place furniture or shelving across the room	**do** keep all doors open to 'borrow' space **don't** add screens or partitions **don't** place window boxes outside rooms with patchy natural light	**do** keep things simple; these rooms and windows will look their best when decorated with a light touch **don't** complicate rooms with screens, partitions or bed canopies
bland	**do** add interesting textures **do** introduce shiny, sparkly and reflective surfaces **don't** overload the room with patterns or styles **don't** use wallpaper unless the print is tiny and discreet **don't** use strong, saturated colour on walls	**do** show off a show-stopping piece of furniture or a painting against one of the shorter walls **do** use strong, saturated colour or bold wallpaper, but only on the shorter walls **don't** adopt a cluttered, eclectic style	**do** go easy on vibrant, eclectic styles **do** use wallpaper, but stick to small repeat patterns, and avoid geometric designs **don't** paint walls with strong, saturated colour; add interest with artworks or ornaments
cold	**do** aim to light all four corners to increase size; add pools of intimate tungsten light to create warmth **don't** paint ceilings a warm shade to lower them **don't** use saturated colours on walls; choose pale, warm shades	**do** use warm, saturated colours on short walls, but combine with pale neutrals on the longer ones **do** add a mid-toned shade to avoid the stark contrast of very pale and very dark objects **do** make a focal point of fireplaces	**do** choose warm paint tones, but keep them pale; use the same shade for walls and ceiling **do** create symmetrical displays, and incorporate tactile textures **don't** lower ceilings by painting them a darker shade
dated	**do** cut down on clutter; give remaining objects breathing space **do** darken wood floors, but give them a glossy finish **don't** create a focal point of strong wall colour **don't** introduce large patterns, and limit smaller ones	**do** create a strong focal point on a shorter wall **do** darken wood floors, but give them a high gloss finish **do** choose plain flooring in a neutral shade	**do** create symmetrical arrangements **do** paint walls in pale colours rather than advancing, saturated shades **don't** darken wooden floors; the contrast will illuminate irregularities

	low-ceilinged	dark	overlooked
small	**do** use uplighters to give the illusion of added height and space **do** drop dado height and shorten skirting boards **do** use full-length curtains **don't** use vertical stripes	**do** make use of shiny and reflective surfaces **do** soften dark furniture with pale cushions or throws **don't** use either advancing wall colours or receding shades that are very pale; opt for a middle ground that makes dark rooms warmer and less gloomy	**do** dress windows in a pared-down, simple style **don't** cover beds with a canopy or curtains **don't** place furniture or shelving across the room
narrow	**do** paint ceilings white or a very pale shade **do** create a strong focal point on a short wall **don't** use vertical stripes	**do** boost daylight levels with halogen bulbs **do** use reflective and sparkly surfaces **do** lay pale, neutral flooring **don't** add screens or partitions	**do** keep all doors open to 'borrow' space **don't** add screens or partitions **don't** place window boxes outside rooms with patchy natural light
misshapen	**do** use wallpaper, but avoid designs with horizontal stripes **do** paint walls, skirting boards and ceilings the same pale shade **don't** decorate with vertical stripes	**do** paint the area above the picture rail a pale receding colour **do** boost low daylight with various artificial lights **don't** paint the entire room a pale colour; paint one wall a richer shade	**do** keep things simple; these rooms and windows will look their best when decorated with a light touch **don't** complicate rooms with screens, partitions or bed canopies
low-ceilinged		**do** add plenty of artificial light; include uplighters to raise the apparent height of low rooms **do** fit full-length curtains; make sure they don't obscure the window when drawn; avoid light-absorbing dark or matt fabrics	**do** lengthen curtains and sheers to create an illusion of height **do** paint ceilings white to maximize height and light **don't** cover your bed with a canopy or curtains **don't** raise the height of your windows
dark	**do** add plenty of artificial light; include uplighters to raise the apparent height of low rooms **do** fit full-length curtains; make sure they don't obscure the window when drawn; avoid light-absorbing dark or matt fabrics		**do** cover windows with the bare minimum; keep curtains and blinds clear of windowpanes by day **don't** place window boxes or pots on windowsills **don't** screen off areas of the room with partitions or curtains
overlooked	**do** lengthen curtains and sheers to create an illusion of height **do** paint ceilings white to maximize height and light **don't** cover your bed with a canopy or curtains **don't** raise the height of your windows	**do** cover windows with the bare minimum; keep curtains and blinds clear of windowpanes by day **don't** place window boxes or pots on windowsills **don't** screen off areas of the room with partitions or curtains	
bland	**do** use wallpaper, avoiding large, overbearing designs **don't** be heavy-handed with strong, saturated colour; paint a single wall only, or add colour with artworks, fabrics or accessories **don't** hang oversized mirrors or vast artworks	**do** use sparkly and reflective surfaces **don't** use strong, saturated colour; keep to mid-toned warm shades **don't** choose dramatic curtains if they obscure any part of the window	**do** opt for a show-stopping window treatment **do** cocoon yourself with canopied beds and decorative screens **do** add colourful window boxes and potted plants
cold	**do** add vertical stripes; choose warm, earthy tones **do** choose a combination of uplighters for height and tungsten lamps for warmth **don't** darken the area above the picture rail; paint walls, wainscot and ceilings in a pale but warm neutral	**do** paint rooms in mid-toned warm shades **do** choose tungsten light for warmth, but add halogen spots for additional daytime lighting **do** install frosted-glass partitions, but soften them with warm, earthy shades on solid walls	**do** add piles of cushions, throws and a canopy over the bed; make cavernous spaces cosier by placing a sofa or shelves across the room **don't** block daylight with fussy nets or gathered sheers; soften a minimal look with warm, full-length curtains
dated	**do** paint skirting boards the same colour as the walls **do** choose full-length curtains **don't** fit deep skirting boards and cornicing	**do** darken wood floors, but give them a high-gloss finish **do** replace solid partition walls with frosted glass **do** introduce shiny and reflective surfaces	**do** avoid fussy gathered sheers and net curtains **do** dress windows in a simple modern style; bold pattern will add interest in place of swags and gathers **don't** place mirrors so that passers-by receive an even greater view

	bland	cold	dated
small	**do** add interesting textures **do** introduce shiny, sparkly and reflective surfaces **don't** overload the room with patterns or styles **don't** use wallpaper unless the print is tiny and discreet **don't** use strong, saturated colour on walls	**do** aim to light all four corners to increase size; add pools of intimate tungsten light to create warmth **don't** paint ceilings a warm shade to lower them **don't** use saturated colours on walls; choose pale, warm shades	**do** cut down on clutter; give remaining objects breathing space **do** darken wood floors, but give them a glossy finish **don't** create a focal point of strong wall colour **don't** introduce large patterns, and limit smaller ones
narrow	**do** show off a show-stopping piece of furniture or a painting against one of the shorter walls **do** use strong, saturated colour or bold wallpaper, but only on the shorter walls **don't** adopt a cluttered, eclectic style	**do** use warm, saturated colours on short walls, but combine with pale neutrals on the longer ones **do** add a mid-toned shade to avoid the stark contrast of very pale and very dark objects **do** make a focal point of fireplaces	**do** create a strong focal point on a shorter wall **do** darken wood floors, but give them a high gloss finish **do** choose plain flooring in a neutral shade
misshapen	**do** go easy on vibrant, eclectic styles **do** use wallpaper, but stick to small repeat patterns, and avoid geometric designs **don't** paint walls with strong, saturated colour; add interest with artworks or ornaments	**do** choose warm paint tones, but keep them pale; use the same shade for walls and ceiling **do** create symmetrical displays, and incorporate tactile textures **don't** lower ceilings by painting them a darker shade	**do** create symmetrical arrangements **do** paint walls in pale colours rather than advancing, saturated shades **don't** darken wooden floors; the contrast will illuminate irregularities
low-ceilinged	**do** use wallpaper, avoiding large, overbearing designs **don't** be heavy-handed with strong, saturated colour; paint a single wall only, or add colour with artworks, fabrics or accessories **don't** hang oversized mirrors or vast artworks	**do** add vertical stripes; choose warm, earthy tones **do** choose a combination of uplighters for height and tungsten lamps for warmth **don't** darken the area above the picture rail; paint walls, wainscot and ceilings in a pale but warm neutral	**do** paint skirting boards the same colour as the walls **do** choose full-length curtains **don't** fit deep skirting boards and cornicing
dark	**do** use sparkly and reflective surfaces **don't** use strong, saturated colour; keep to mid-toned warm shades **don't** choose dramatic curtains if they obscure any part of the window	**do** paint rooms in mid-toned warm shades **do** choose tungsten light for warmth, but add halogen spots for additional daytime lighting **do** install frosted-glass partitions, but soften them with warm, earthy shades on solid walls	**do** darken wood floors, but give them a high-gloss finish **do** replace solid partition walls with frosted glass **do** introduce shiny and reflective surfaces
overlooked	**do** opt for a show-stopping window treatment **do** cocoon yourself with canopied beds and decorative screens **do** add colourful window boxes and potted plants	**do** add piles of cushions, throws and a canopy over the bed; make cavernous spaces cosier by placing a sofa or shelves across the room **don't** block daylight with fussy nets or gathered sheers; soften a minimal look with warm, full-length curtains	**do** avoid fussy gathered sheers and net curtains **do** dress windows in a simple modern style; bold pattern will add interest in place of swags and gathers **don't** place mirrors so that passers-by receive an even greater view
bland		**do** add saturated colour in warm, earthy tones (avoid very dark shades because they absorb too much light) **do** create interest and warmth with pools of tungsten light **do** make fireplaces a focal point	**do** find a halfway point between cluttered and bland; decorate surfaces with a few large modern objects or group ornaments to create a cohesive display **don't** obliterate character; add some bright colour or wallpaper, or retain some old favourite pieces
cold	**do** add saturated colour in warm, earthy tones (avoid very dark shades because they absorb too much light) **do** create interest and warmth with pools of tungsten light **do** make fireplaces a focal point		**do** paint walls in warm, earthy tones **do** install both warming tungsten lamps and contemporary halogen spots **do** darken wood floors but give them a high-gloss finish; don't darken the area above picture rails
dated	**do** find a halfway point between cluttered and bland; decorate surfaces with a few large, modern objects or group ornaments to create a cohesive display **don't** obliterate character; add some bright colour or wallpaper, or retain some old favourite pieces	**do** paint walls in warm, earthy tones **do** install both warming tungsten lamps and contemporary halogen spots **do** darken wood floors but give them a high-gloss finish; don't darken the area above picture rails	

sources

The Alternative Flooring Company
01264 335111 for stockists
www.alternative-flooring.co.uk
Natural flooring products.

Armitage Shanks
Armitage
Rugeley
Staffordshire WS15 4BT
01543 490253
www.armitage-shanks.co.uk
Bathroom fixtures.

Baileys Home & Garden
The Engine Shed
Station Approach
Ross-on-Wye
Herefordshire HR9 7BW
01989 561931
www.baileyshomeand garden.com
Wide range of home accessories by mail.

Bulthaup
37 Wigmore Street
London W1U 1PN
020 7495 3663 for stockists
www.bulthaup.com
Contemporary kitchen furniture.

The Conran Shop
Michelin House
81 Fulham Road
London SW3 6RD
020 7589 7401
www.conran.co.uk
Contemporary furniture, storage and accessories.

C.P. Hart
213 Newnham Terrace
Hercules Road
London SE1 7DR
020 7902 1000
www.cphart.co.uk
Modern bathrooms.

Decorative Living
55 New Kings Road
London SW6 4SE
020 7736 5623
Antiques.

Designers Guild
267–271 & 275–277
King's Road
London SW3 5EN
020 7351 5775 for store
020 7243 7300 for stockists and mail order
www.designersguild.com
Contemporary paint colours; inspiring fabrics and wallpapers.

DR Services (London)
Plumpton House
Plumpton Road
Hoddesdon
Hertfordshire EN11 0LB
01992 447122
www.drservices.co.uk
Made-to-measure sliding glass and timber doors.

Dulux Customer Care Centre
01753 550 555
www.dulux.co.uk
Useful paint advice and colour-matching service.

Easy
31 West Bowling Street
Edinburgh EH6 5NX
0131 554 7077
www.easy-arch-salv.co.uk
Architectural antiques.

Farrow & Ball
Uddens Estate
Wimborne
Dorset BH21 7NL
01202 876141
www.farrow-ball.com
Great range of paints.

First Floor Fulham
174 Wandsworth Bridge Rd
London SW6 2UQ
020 7736 1123
www.firstfloor.co.uk
Dalsouple rubber, linoleum, vinyl, wood, natural fibres.

Forbes & Lomax
205a St John's Hill
London SW11 1TH
020 7738 0202
www.forbesandlomax.co.uk
Switches, sockets and dimmers.

General Trading Company
2 Symons Street
London SW3 2TJ
020 7730 0411
www.generaltrading.co.uk
Furniture, antiques and accessories.

Habitat
196 Tottenham Court Road
London W1T 9LD
020 7631 3880
www.habitat.net
Home accessories and furniture.

The Hardwood Flooring Company
146–52 West End Lane
London NW6 1SD
020 7328 8481
www.hardwoodflooring company.com
Wooden flooring.

Heal's
196 Tottenham Court Road
London W1T 7LQ
020 7636 1666
www.heals.co.uk
Contemporary furniture, accessories and storage.

The Holding Company
241–45 King's Road
London SW3 5EL
020 7352 1600
020 8445 2888 mail order
www.theholdingcompany.co.uk
Storage with style.

Hülsta Furniture
22 Bruton Street
London W1V 6QE
020 7629 4881 stockists
www.huelsta.co.uk
Fitted cabinets for all rooms.

Ian Mankin
109 Regents Park Road
London NW1 8UR
020 7722 0997
Linens and washable cottons in plains, checks and stripes.

Ikea
Brent Park
2 Drury Way
255 North Circular Road
London NW13 OJQ
0845 355 1141
www.ikea.co.uk
Kitchen units, furniture and storage

The Iron Bed Company
Call 01243 380 600 or visit www.ironbed.co.uk for stores
Beds, including iron bedheads.

John Cullen Lighting
585 Kings Road
London SW6 2EH
020 7371 5400
www.johncullenlighting.co.uk
Discreet fittings and a design service

John Lewis
Oxford Street
London W1A 1EX
020 7629 7711 for stores and information
www.johnlewis.com
Department stores with everything for the home.

Knobs & Knockers
567 Kings Road
London SW6 2EB
020 7384 2884
www.knobs-and-knockers.com
Modern and period knobs, grilles and window fittings.

LASSCO
41 Maltby Street
London SE1 3PA
020 7394 2102
www.lassco.co.uk
Architectural salvage.

Nu-Line
305–17 Westbourne Park Road
London W11 1EF
020 7727 7748
www.nu-line.net
Architectural ironmongery.

Papers & Paints
4 Park Walk
London SW10 OAD
020 7352 8626
www.colourman.com
Wide range of paint colours; samples colour-matched.

Pellfold Parthos
1 The Quadrant
Howarth Road
Maidenhead
Berkshire SL6 1AP
01628 773353
www.design4space.com
Solid and glass partitions for large spaces.

The Pier
200–203 Tottenham Court Road
London W1T 7PL
020 7637 7001
www.pier.co.uk
Furniture, storage and accessories.

Plasti-Kote
01223 836400 for stockists
www.spraypaint.co.uk
Easy-to-apply decorative finishes.

Poggenpohl
0800 243781 for stockists
www.poggenpohl.de
Custom-designed fitted kitchen furniture.

Preedy Glass
Lamb Works
North Road
London N7 9DP
020 7700 0377
www.preedyglass.com
Interior glass doors from made-to-measure glass specialists

The Rug Company
124 Holland Park Avenue
London W11 4UE
020 7229 5148
www.rugcompany.co.uk
Traditional and modern floor coverings.

The Shutter Shop
2–8 Chelsea Harbour
London SW10 OXE
020 7351 4204
www.shuttershop.org
Louvre shutters and venetian blinds.

SKK Lighting
34 Lexington Street
London W1F OLH
020 7434 4095
www.skk.net
Modern lighting.

Sottini
The Bathroom Works
National Avenue
Kingston upon Hull
HU5 4HS
01482 449513
www.sottini.co.uk
Bathroom fixtures.

Shaker
72–73 Marylebone High Street
London W1U 5JW
020 7935 9461
Shaker-style furniture.

Smeg
08708 243781 for stockists and information.
www.smeguk.com
Stainless-steel kitchen appliances.

Sofa Workshop
01443 238699 for your nearest branch.
www.sofaworkshop.co.uk
Sofas and armchairs.

Tidmarsh & Sons
01707 886226 for a brochure and samples
All types of blinds.

Velux
Woodside Way
Glenrothes East
Fife KY7 4ND
0870 1667676
www.velux.co.uk
Roof windows.

picture credits

Key: ph = photographer, **a** = above, **b** = below, **r** = right, **l** = left, **c** = centre.

Page **1** ph Debi Treloar/Susan Cropper's family home in London. www.63hlg.com; **2–3** ph David Montgomery/an apartment in New York designed by Ken Foreman; **4al** ph Jan Baldwin/Clare Mosley's house in London; **4ar** ph Tom Leighton; **4cl** ph Alan Williams/architect Eric Liftin's own apartment in New York; **4cr** ph Henry Bourne; **4bl** ph Polly Wreford/Kimberley Watson's house in London; **4br** ph Andrew Wood/Chelsea Loft apartment in New York, designed by The Moderns; **5a** ph Jan Baldwin/Jan Hashey and Yasuo Minagawa; **5c** ph Chris Everard/Adèle Lakhdari's home in Milan; **5b** ph Chris Everard/Yuen-Wei Chew's apartment in London designed by Paul Daly Design Studio Ltd; **7** ph Polly Wreford/Carol Reid's apartment in Paris; **8–9** ph Jan Baldwin/Sophie Eadie's family home in London; **11** ph Debi Treloar/Kristiina Ratia and Jeff Gocke's family home in Norwalk, Connecticut; **12–13** ph Alan Williams/Louise Robbins' house in North West Herefordshire; **14** ph Jan Baldwin/a house in New York designed by Brendan Coburn and Joseph Smith from Coburn Architecture; **15** ph Chris Everard/ photographer Guy Hills' house in London designed by Joanna Rippon and Maria Speake of Retrouvius; **16l** ph Jan Baldwin/a house in New York designed by Brendan Coburn and Joseph Smith from Coburn Architecture; **16ar** ph Chris Everard/the London apartment of the Sheppard Day Design Partnership; **16b** ph Ray Main/Central London apartment designed by Ben Kelly Design, 1999; **17al** ph Jan Baldwin; **17ar** ph Chris Everard/Mark Weinstein's apartment in New York designed by Lloyd Schwan; **17bl** ph Andrew Wood/Michael Asplund's apartment in Stockholm, Sweden; **17br** ph Chris Everard/Peter and Nicole Dawes' apartment, designed by Mullman Seidman Architects; **18al** ph Chris Everard/architect Jonathan Clark's home in London; **18ar** & **18bl** ph Chris Everard/interior designer Ann Boyd's own apartment in London; **18br** ph Andrew Wood/Christer Wallensteen's apartment in Stockholm, Sweden; **19bl** ph Polly Wreford/Adria Ellis' apartment in New York; **19c** ph Polly Wreford/Mary Foley's house in Connecticut; **19ar** ph Catherine Gratwicke/Laura Stoddart's apartment in London; **19br** ph Ray Main/a loft in London designed by Nico Rensch, lighting by SKK; **20al** ph Chris Everard/Lisa & Richard Frisch's apartment in New York designed by Patricia Seidman of Mullman Seidman Architects, interior decoration by Mariette Himes Gomez; **20bl** ph Chris Everard/architect Jonathan Clark's home in London; **20–21** ph Debi Treloar/the designer couple Tea Bendix & Tobias Jacobsen's home, Denmark; **22a** ph Debi Treloar/Mark and Sally of Baileys Home and Garden's house in Herefordshire; **22b** ph Chris Everard/the London apartment of the Sheppard Day Design Partnership; **23al** ph Chris Everard/Ben Atfield's house in London; **23ac** ph Polly Wreford/Ros Fairman's house in London; **23ar** ph Chris Everard/a London apartment designed by architect Gavin Jackson; **23bl** ph Andrew Wood/Andrew Duncanson's (owner of Modernity) apartment in Stockholm, Sweden; **23br** ph Debi Treloar/Mark and Sally of Baileys Home and Garden's house in Herefordshire; **24l** ph Chris Everard/Mark Weinstein's apartment in New York designed by Lloyd Schwan; **24–25**a ph Chris Everard/Nadav Kander & Nicole Verity's house; **24–25b** ph Polly Wreford/Lena Proudlock's house in Gloucestershire; **25ar** ph Jan Baldwin/Sophie Eadie's family home in London; **25br** ph Chris Everard/Bob & Maureen Macris' apartment on Fifth Avenue in New York designed by Sage Wimer Coombe Architects; **26al** ph Chris Everard/an apartment in Milan designed by Tito Canella of Canella & Achilli Architects; **26b** ph Chris Everard/a house in London designed by Helen Ellery of The Plot London; **26–27a** ph Chris Everard/architect Jonathan Clark's home in London; **27ar** ph Chris Everard/Jo Warman – Interior Concepts; **27bl** ph Andrew Wood/Vanessa & Robert Fairer's studio in London designed by Woolf Architects 020 7428 9500; **27br** ph Jan Baldwin/Mona Nerenberg and Lisa Bynon's house in Sag Harbor; **28al** ph Tom Leighton/Roger & Fay Oates' house in Herefordshire; **28ac** ph Alan Williams/the Arbuthnott family's house near Cirencester designed by Nicholas Arbuthnott, fabrics designed by Vanessa Arbuthnott; **28bc** ph Polly Wreford/Ann Shore's former house in London; **28–29** ph Chris Everard/Mark Weinstein's apartment in New York designed by Lloyd Schwan; 29ac ph Polly Wreford/ Kimberley Watson's house in London; **29bc** ph Polly Wreford/Clare Nash's house in London; **29ar** ph Catherine Gratwicke/Francesca Mills' house in London – 70s scarf cushions from Maisonette; **29br** ph David Montgomery/Sasha Waddell's house in London; **30** ph Chris Everard/a house in London designed by Helen Ellery of The Plot London; **31** ph Debi Treloar/the home of Patty Collister in London, owner of An Angel At My Table; **32l** ph Chris Everard/Ben Atfield's house in London; **32ar** ph Chris Everard/an apartment in Milan designed by Tito Canella of Canella & Achilli Architects; **32br** ph Debi Treloar/ Clare and David Mannix-Andrews' house, Hove, East Sussex; **33al** ph Chris Everard/a house in London designed by Helen Ellery of The Plot London; **33bl** ph Debi Treloar/North London flat of presentation skills trainer/actress and her teacher husband, designed by Gordana Mandic of buildburo; **33ar** ph Christopher Drake/Andrea Spencer's house in London; **33br** ph Andrew Wood/Rosa Dean & Ed Baden-Powell's apartment in London, designed by Urban Salon 020 7357 8800; **34** ph Debi Treloar/Julia & David O'Driscoll's house in London; **35a** ph Debi Treloar/Clare and David Mannix-Andrews' house, Hove, East Sussex; **35b** ph Debi Treloar/Wim and Josephine's apartment in Amsterdam; **36a** ph Polly Wreford/home of 27.12 Design Ltd., Chelsea, NYC; **36b** ph Debi Treloar/the home of Patty Collister in London, owner of An Angel At My Table; **37l** ph Ray Main/a house in East Hampton, interior by Vicente Wolf; **37ar** ph Debi Treloar/a family home in London, portraits by artist Julian Opie, Lisson Gallery; **37br** ph Debi Treloar/Nicky Phillips' apartment in London; **38** ph Debi Treloar/Anna Massee of Het Grote Avontuur (The Great Adventure)'s home in Amsterdam; **39a** Alan Williams/Louise Robbins' house in North West Herefordshire; **39b** ph Polly Wreford/Daniel Jasiak's apartment in Paris; **40al** ph Ray Main/Jamie Falla's house in London designed by MOOArc; **40bl** ph Debi Treloar/Susan Cropper's family home in London. www.63hlg.com; **40ar** ph Polly Wreford/Clare Nash's house in London; **40br** ph Chris Everard/Ben Atfield's house in London; **41** ph Chris Everard/ Simon Brignall & Christina Rosetti's loft apartment in London designed by David Mikhail Architects; **42al**, **acl**, **bl**, **ac**, **bc** all ph James Merrell; **42bcl** Simon Upton; **42r**, **43al** & **bl** ph Tom Leighton; **43ar** ph Jan Baldwin; **43br** ph Jan Baldwin/Jan Hashey and Yasuo Minagawa; **44** ph Henry Bourne; **45** ph Jan Baldwin/the Campbell family's apartment in London, architecture by Voon Wong Architects; **46al** ph Chris Everard/Ben Atfield's house in London; **46ar** ph Henry Bourne; **46b** both ph Chris Everard/a house in London designed by Helen Ellery of The Plot London; **47al** ph Christopher Drake/William Yeoward & Colin Orchard's home in London; **47ar** ph Alan Williams/the Norfolk home of Geoff & Gilly Newberry of Bennison Fabrics – Pondicherry fabric by Bennison; **47bl** ph Tom Leighton/paint Farrow & Ball: floor Mouse's Back floor paint no. 40, cupboards Green Smoke no. 47 and interior Red Fox no. 48, walls & woodwork String no. 8, ceiling Off White no. 3; **47br** ph Chris Everard/a house in London designed by Helen Ellery of The Plot London; **48a** ph Debi Treloar/Morag Myerscough's house in Clerkenwell, London – her house gallery/shop; **48b** ph Debi Treloar/a London apartment designed by James Soane and Christopher Ash of Project Orange; **49al** ph Christopher Drake/Vivien Lawrence an interior designer in London (020 8209 0562); **49bl** ph Jan Baldwin/the Campbell family's apartment in London, architecture by Voon Wong Architects; **49ar** ph Debi Treloar/Nicky Phillips' apartment in London; **49br** ph Jan Baldwin/Clare Mosley's house in London; **50a** ph Jan Baldwin/architect Joseph Dirand's apartment in Paris; **50b** ph Jan Baldwin/a house in New York designed by Brendan Coburn and Joseph Smith from Coburn Architecture; **50–51** ph Chris Everard/Jo Warman – Interior Concepts; **52l** ph Jan Baldwin/ Sophie Eadie's family home in London; 52ar Jan Baldwin/Mark Smith's home in the Cotswolds; **52br** ph Debi Treloar/Clare and David Mannix-Andrews' house, Hove, East Sussex; **53al&bl** ph Debi Treloar/ Susan Cropper's family home in London. www.63hlg.com; **53ac** ph Debi Treloar; **53ar** ph Alan Williams/ the Norfolk home of Geoff & Gilly Newberry of Bennison Fabrics – Daisy Chain wallpaper by Bennison; **53c** both ph Catherine Gratwicke; **53bc** & **53br** ph Polly Wreford/Emma Greenhill's London home; **54** ph Henry Bourne; **55** ph Polly Wreford/Sawmill Studios; **56l** ph Ray Main/Seth Stein's house in London, wall light by Serge Mouille; **56ar** ph Ray Main/Arteluce light from Atrium; **56br** ph Christopher Drake/ Vivien Lawrence an interior designer in London (020 8209 0562); **57al** ph Simon Upton; **57bl** ph Alan Williams/Alannah Weston's house in London designed by Stickland Coombe Architecture; **57r** ph James Merrell; **58a** ph Polly Wreford/Kimberley Watson's house in London; **58bl** ph Andrew Wood/a house in London designed by Guy Stansfeld 020 7727 0133; **58br** ph Chris Everard/Charles Bateson's house in London; **59** ph Chris Everard/interior designer Angela Kearsey's house in London – architectural design by Dols Wong Architects, interior design by Angela Kearsey; **60** ph Andrew Wood/Richard and Sue Hare's house in Idaho designed by Mark Pynn A.I.A. of McMillen Pynn Architecture L.L.P.; **61a** ph Henry Bourne; **61bl** ph Ray Main/Mark Jennings' apartment in New York designed by Asfour Guzy; **61br** ph Chris Everard/Ian Chee of VX design & architecture; **62al** ph Tom Leighton; **62bl** ph Polly Wreford/ Lena Proudlock's house in Gloucestershire; **62r** ph Chris Everard; **62–63** ph Polly Wreford/Sawmill Studios; **63ac** ph Polly Wreford/Louise Jackson's house in London; **63bc** ph Polly Wreford/Clare Nash's house in London; **63ar** ph Debi Treloar/Rudi, Melissa & Archie Thackry's house in London; **63br** ph James Merrell; **64** ph James Merrell/Janie Jackson, stylist and designer; **65** ph Chris Everard/ Programmable House in London, designed by d-squared; **66al** ph James Merrell/Janie Jackson, stylist and designer; **66ar** ph Chris Everard/Programmable House in London, designed by d-squared; **66b** ph Chris Everard/an apartment in London designed by Jo Hagan of Use Architects; 67al ph Polly Wreford/ Mary Foley's house in Connecticut; **67ac** ph Ray Main/Evan Snyderman's house in Brooklyn; **67ar** ph Chris Everard/John Barman's Park Avenue Apartment; **67bl** ph Ray Main/Jonathan Leitersdorf's apartment in New York designed by Jonathan Leitersdorf/Just Design Ltd; **67br** ph Chris Everard/a loft in London designed by Eger Architects; **68** ph Chris Everard/Adèle Lakhdari's home in Milan; **69** both ph Chris Everard/a London apartment designed by architect Gavin Jackson; **70a** ph Chris Everard/Yuen-Wei Chew's apartment in London designed by Paul Daly Design Studio Ltd; **70bl** ph Andrew Wood/Guido Palau's house in North London, designed by Azman Owens Architects; **70br** ph James Merrell; **71al** ph Chris Everard/interior designer Angela Kearsey's house in London – architectural design by Dols Wong Architects, interior design by Angela Kearsey; **71ar** ph Chris Everard/designed by Mullman Seidman

Architects; **71bl** ph Ray Main/Andrea Luria and Zachary Feuer's house in Los Angeles designed by Studio Works, Robert Mangurian and Mary-Ann Ray; **71br** ph Chris Everard/Ian Chee of VX design & architecture; **72** ph Chris Everard/Charles Bateson's house in London; **73al** ph Ray Main/Darren and Sheila Chadwick's apartment in London designed by Sergisson Bates; **73ar** ph Ray Main/Jonathan Reed's apartment in London, lighting designed by Sally Storey, Design Director of John Cullen Lighting; **73b** ph Chris Everard/the Sugarman–Behun house on Long Island; **74al** ph Alan Williams/Donata Sartorio's apartment in Milan; **74ac** & **bc** ph Alan Williams/owner of Gloss, Pascale Bredillet's own apartment in London; **74r** ph Tom Leighton; **74–75** ph Sandra Lane/Harriet Scott of R.K. Alliston's apartment in London; **75ar** ph Alan Williams/Toia Saibene's apartment in Milan; **75cl** ph Christopher Drake/William Yeoward & Colin Orchard's home in London; **75cr** ph Debi Treloar/Annelie Bruijn's home in Amsterdam; **75br** ph Andrew Wood/Mary Shaw's Sequana apartment in Paris; **76** ph Andrew Wood/ an apartment in London designed by Littman Goddard Hogarth Architects; **77** ph Debi Treloar/Kristiina Ratia and Jeff Gocke's family home in Norwalk, Connecticut; **78al** ph James Merrell; **78ar** ph Jan Baldwin/interior designer Didier Gomez's apartment in Paris; **78bl** ph Debi Treloar/designed by Sage Wimer Coombe Architects, New York; **78br** ph Andrew Wood/Johanne Riss' house in Brussels; **79al** ph Andrew Wood/an apartment in London designed by Littman Goddard Hogarth Architects; **79ar** ph Debi Treloar/Nicky Phillips' apartment in London; **79bl** ph Chris Everard/photographer Guy Hills' house in London designed by Joanna Rippon and Maria Speake of Retrouvius; **79br** ph Debi Treloar/Kristiina Ratia and Jeff Gocke's family home in Norwalk, Connecticut; **80–81** ph Andrew Wood/Brian Johnson's apartment in London designed by Johnson Naylor; **81a** ph Chris Everard/Charles Bateson's house in London; **81b** ph Jan Baldwin/Mona Nerenberg and Lisa Bynon's house in Sag Harbor; **82al** ph Chris Everard/Pemper and Rabiner home in New York, designed by David Khouri of Comma; **82ar** ph Debi Treloar/Debi Treloar's family home in north-west London; **82b** ph Ray Main a loft in London designed by Nico Rensch, light from SKK; **83al** ph Debi Treloar/an apartment in New York designed by Steven Learner Studio; **83ar** ph Jan Baldwin/interior designer Didier Gomez's apartment in Paris; **83bl** ph Jan Baldwin/the Fitzwilliam-Lay's family home. Architecture by Totem Design, interior design by Henri Fitzwilliam-Lay and Totem Design; **83br** ph Chris Everard/Garden Room, London for David & Anne Harriss designed by Eger Architects; **84al** ph Andrew Wood/Michael Benevento – Orange Group; **84c** ph Andrew Wood/Nicki De Metz's flat in London designed by De Metz architects; **84bl** ph Jan Baldwin/ architect Joseph Dirand's apartment in Paris; **84–85** ph Debi Treloar/Kristiina Ratia and Jeff Gocke's family home in Norwalk, Connecticut; **85ac** ph Chris Everard/Sig.ra Venturini's apartment in Milan; **85ar** ph James Merrell; **85bl** ph Jan Baldwin/Constanze von Unruh's house in London; **85bcl** ph Debi Treloar; **85bcr** ph Henry Bourne; **85br** ph Debi Treloar/Annelie Bruijn's home in Amsterdam; **85** details: **a** & **b** ph David Montgomery, **c** ph James Merrell; **86** & **87** ph Polly Wreford/Kimberley Watson's house in London; **88al** ph Debi Treloar/new build house in Notting Hill designed by Seth Stein Architects; **88r** ph Debi Treloar/Sudi Pigott's house in London; **88bl** ph Debi Treloar/Sarah Munro and Brian Ayling's home in London; **89al** ph Jan Baldwin/Emma Wilson's house in London; **89bl** ph Debi Treloar/the home of Studio Aandacht. Design by Ben Lambers; **89ar** ph Debi Treloar/Cristine Tholstrup Hermansen and Helge Drenck's house in Copenhagen; **89br** ph Polly Wreford/Ann Shore's former house in London; **90a** ph Catherine Gratwicke/Lucy and Marc Salem's London home-painting by Rachael Garfield, velvet cushions with tassel trim by Lucy Salem; **90b** ph Debi Treloar/designed by Sage Wimer Coombe Architects, New York; **90–91** ph Debi Treloar/Catherine Chermayeff & Jonathan David's family home in New York, designed by Asfour Guzy Architects; **92** ph Debi Treloar/Vincent & Frieda Plasschaert's house in Brugge, Belgium; **93al** ph Polly Wreford/Daniel Jasiak's apartment in Paris; **93ar** ph Debi Treloar/Sudi Pigott's house in London; **93bl** ph Debi Treloar/Victoria Andreae's house in London; **93br** Rose Hammick's home in London – armoir from Mark Maynard Antiques, antique toile panel from Nicole Fabre Antiques; **94a** ph Debi Treloar/Mark and Sally of Baileys Home and Garden's house in Herefordshire; **94b** ph Tom Leighton; **94–95** ph Debi Treloar/designed by Ash Sakula Architects; **96al, ar** & **bl** ph Polly Wreford/ Kimberley Watson's house in London; **96acr** & **br** ph Polly Wreford; **96bcr** ph Catherine Gratwicke; **96–97** ph Alan Williams/architect Eric Liftin's own apartment in New York; **97ac** ph Polly Wreford/an apartment in New York designed by Belmont Freeman Architects; **97bc** ph Alan Williams/owner of Gloss, Pascale Bredillet's own apartment in London; **97ar** ph Polly Wreford/Glenn Carwithen & Sue Miller's house in London; **97br** ph Polly Wreford/Ros Fairman's house in London; **98** ph Ray Main/ Lee F. Mindel's apartment in New York, lighting designed by Johnson Schwinghammer, light from Mobilier; **99** ph Debi Treloar/Mark and Sally of Baileys Home and Garden's house in Herefordshire; **100al** ph Ray Main/Greg Yale's house in Southampton, NY; **100r** ph Fritz von der Schulenburg/Piero Castellini Baldissera's house in Montalcino, Siena; **100bl** ph Andrew Wood/Kurt Bredenbeck's apartment at the Barbican, London; **101al** ph Polly Wreford/Mary Foley's house in Connecticut; **101ac** ph James Merrell; **101ar** ph Jan Baldwin/Constanze von Unruh's house in London; **101bl** ph Debi Treloar/Susan Cropper's family home in London. www.63hlg.com; **101br** ph Ray Main/Lee F. Mindel's apartment in New York, lighting designed by Johnson Schwinghammer, light from Mobilier; **102–103** ph Alan Williams/Warner Johnson's apartment in New York designed by Edward Cabot of Cabot Design Ltd;

103a ph Chris Everard/Charles Bateson's house in London; **103b** ph Alan Williams/Andrew Wallace's house in London; **104al** ph Chris Everard/a house in Paris designed by Bruno Tanquerel; **104bl** ph Jan Baldwin/art dealer Gul Coskun's apartment in London; **104ar** ph Debi Treloar/Mark and Sally of Baileys Home and Garden's house in Herefordshire; **104br** ph Alan Williams/Louise Robbins' house in North West Herefordshire; **105, 106al** & **106bl** ph James Merrell; **106r** ph Debi Treloar; **106–107a** ph James Merrell/Janie Jackson, stylist and designer; **107ac** ph James Merrell; **107ar** Chris Tubbs/Mike and Deborah Geary's beach house in Dorset; **107bl** ph Andrew Wood/Philip and Barbara Silver's house in Idaho designed by Mark Pynn A.I.A. of McMillen Pynn Architecture L.L.P.; **107bc** ph Andrew Wood/ Mary Shaw's Sequana apartment in Paris; **107br** ph Alan Williams/New York apartment designed by Bruce Bierman; **108** ph Polly Wreford/Mary Foley's house in Connecticut; **109** ph Tom Leighton; **110al** ph Chris Everard; **110ar** ph Polly Wreford/Clare Nash's house in London; **110bl** ph Ray Main; **110br** ph Andrew Wood/Roger and Suzy Black's apartment in London designed by Johnson Naylor; **111al** ph Tom Leighton; **111ac** ph Chris Everard/François Muracciole's apartment in Paris; **111ar** ph Jan Baldwin/ Constanze von Unruh's house in London; **111bl** ph Alan Williams/Toia Saibene's apartment in Milan; **111br** ph Andrew Wood/Century 020 7487 5100; **112al** ph Andrew Wood/Chelsea Loft apartment in New York, designed by The Moderns; **112ar** ph Debi Treloar/artist David Hopkins' house in East London, designed by Yen-Yen Teh of Emulsion; **112b** ph Tom Leighton; **113** ph Debi Treloar/Catherine Chermayeff & Jonathan David's family home in New York, designed by Asfour Guzy Architects; **114** ph Alan Williams/the Arbuthnott family's house near Cirencester designed by Nicholas Arbuthnott, fabrics designed by Vanessa Arbuthnott; **115al** ph Debi Treloar/Morag Myerscough's house in Clerkenwell, London – her house gallery/shop; **115ar** ph Chris Everard/an apartment in Milan designed by Tito Canella of Canella & Achilli Architects; **115b** ph Debi Treloar/Imogen Chapel's home in Suffolk; **116al** ph Andrew Wood; **116cl** ph Tham Nhu-Tran; **116b** all details ph Andrew Wood; **116c** ph Polly Wreford/ home of 27.12 Design Ltd., Chelsea, NYC; **116r** & **116–117** ph Tom Leighton; **117a** ph Polly Wreford/ Kimberley Watson's house in London; **117b** ph Polly Wreford/Mary Foley's house in Connecticut; **118–119** ph Tom Leighton.

business credits

27.12 Design Ltd
333 Hudson Street
10th Floor
New York, NY 10014, USA
+ 1 212 727 8169
www.2712design.com
Pages **36a, 116c.**

www.63hlg.com
Pages **1, 40bl, 53al, 53bl, 101bl.**

An Angel At My Table
116A Fortess Road
London NW5 2HL
020 7424 9777
and 14 High Street
Saffron Walden
Essex CB10 1AY
01799 528777
Painted furniture.
Pages **31, 36b.**

Angela Kearsey Designs
General interior design and decoration
020 7483 0967
Angela.Kearsey@btinternet.com
Pages **59, 71al.**

Ann Boyd Design
33 Elystan Place
London SW3 3NT
Pages **18ar, 18bl.**

Ann Shore, Designer, Stylist and Owner of Story
Story
4 Wilkes Street
Spitalfields
London E1 6QF
020 7377 0313
story@btconnect.com
Personal selection of old and new furniture and accessories.
Pages **28bc, 89br.**

Annelie Bruijn
Annelie_bruijn@email.com
+ 31 653 702869
Pages **75cr, 85br.**

Asfour Guzy Architects
+ 1 212 334 9350
easfour@asfourguzy.com
Pages **61bl, 90–91, 113.**

Ash Sakula Architects
24 Rosebery Avenue
London EC1R 4SX
020 7837 9735
www.ashsak.com
Pages **94–95.**

Asplund (showroom and shop)
Sibyllegatan 31
114 42 Stockholm
Sweden
+ 46 8 662 52 84
Page **17bl.**

Azman Associates (formerly
Azman Owens Architects)
18 Charlotte Road
London EC2A 3PB
020 7739 8191
www.azmanowens.com
Page **70bl.**

Baileys Home & Garden
The Engine Shed
Station Approach
Ross-on-Wye
Herefordshire HR9 7BW
01989 563015
www.baileyshomeand
garden.com
Pages **22a, 23br, 94a, 99,
104ar.**

behun/ziff design
153 East 53rd Street
43rd Floor
New York, NY 10022, USA
+ 1 212 292 6233
Page **73b.**

Belmont Freeman Architects
110 West 40th Street
New York, NY 10018, USA
+ 1 212 382 3311
Page **97ac.**

Ben Kelly Design
10 Stoney Street
London SE1 9AD
020 7378 8116
bkduk@dircon.co.uk
Page **16b.**

Bennison
16 Holbein Place
London SW1W 8NL
020 7730 8076
www.bennisonfabrics.com
Pages **47ar, 53ar.**

Brian Ayling, Artist
020 8802 9853
Page **88bl.**

Bruce Bierman Design
29 West 15th Street
New York, NY 10011, USA
+ 1 212 243 1935
www.biermandesign.com
Page **107br.**

Bruno Tanquerel, Artist
2 Passage St.Sébastien
75011 Paris, France
+ 33 1 43 57 03 93
Page **104al.**

buildburo ltd
7 Tetcott Road
London SW10 0SA
020 7352 1092
www.buildburo.co.uk
Page **33bl.**

Cabot Interior Design
1925 Seventh Avenue
Suite 71
New York, NY 10026, USA
+ 1 212 222 9488
eocabot@aol.com
Pages **102–103.**

Charles Bateson Interior
Design Consultants
18 Kings Road
St Margaret's
Twickenham TW1 2QS
020 8892 3141
charles.bateson@
btinternet.com
Pages **58br, 72, 81a, 103a.**

Circus Architects
Unit 1, Summer Street
London EC1R 5BD
020 7833 1999
Front jacket, above left.

Clare Mosley
Gilding, églomisé panels,
lamps
020 7708 3123
Pages **4al, 49br.**

Clare Nash
House stylist
020 8742 9991
Front jacket above centre,
pages **29bc, 40ar, 63bc,
110ar.**

Coburn Architecture
70 Washington Street
Studio 1001
Brooklyn, NY 11201, USA
+1 718 875 5052
www.coburnarch.com
Pages **14, 16l, 50b.**

Colin Orchard Design
219a Kings Road
London SW3 5EJ
020 7352 2116
Pages **47al, 75cl.**

Constanze von Unruh
Constanze Interior Projects
Richmond, Surrey
020 8948 5533
constanze@constanze
interiorprojects.com
Pages **85bl, 101ar, 111ar.**

Coskun Fine Art London
93 Walton Street
London SW3 2HP
020 7581 9056
www.coskunfineart.com
Page **104bl.**

d-squared design
1 Hatfield House
Baltic Street West
London EC1Y 0ST
020 7253 2240
www.d2-design.co.uk
Pages **65, 66ar.**

Daniel Jasiak, Designer
12 rue Jean Ferrandi
Paris 75006, France
+33 01 45 49 13 56
Pages **39b, 93al.**

David Khouri
Comma Architecture,
Interiors and Furniture
149 Wooster Street
Suite 4NW
New York, NY 10012, USA
+ 1 212 420 7866
www.comma-nyc.com
Page **82al.**

David Mikhail Architects
Unit 29, 1–13 Adler Street
London E1 1EE
020 7377 8424
www.davidmikhail.com
Page **41.**

De Metz Architects
Unit 4, 250 Finchley Road
London NW3 6DN
020 7435 1144
Page **84c.**

Dirand Joseph Architecture
338 rue des Pyrenees
75020 Paris, France
fax +33 01 47 97 78 57
JOSEPH.dirand@
wanadoo.fr
Front jacket centre right,
pages **50a, 84bl.**

Dols Wong Architects
Loft 3, 329 Harrow Road
London W9 3RB
020 7266 2129
dolswong@btinternet.com
Pages **59, 71al.**

Eger Architects, Architects
and landscape architects
2 D'eynsford Road
London SE5 7EB
020 7701 6771
www.egerarchitects.com
Pages **67br, 83br.**

Emma Greenhill
egreenhill@freenet.co.uk
Page **53bc & 53br.**

Emma Wilson
London home available for
photographic shoots:
www.45crossleyst.com
Moroccan home available
for holiday lets:
www.castlesinthesand.com
Page **89al.**

Emulsion
172 Foundling Court
Brunswick Centre
London WC1N 1QE
020 7833 4533
www.emulsionarchitecture.
com
Page **112ar.**

Eric Liftin
Mesh Architecture
Architecture and website
design and development
180 Varick Street
11th Floor
New York, NY 10014, USA
+ 1 212 989 3884
www.mesh-arc.com
Pages **4cl, 96–97.**

Farrow & Ball
www.farrowandball.com
Page **47bl.**

François Muracciole
+ 33 1 43 71 33 03
francois.muracciole@
libertysurf.fr
Page **111ac.**

Gavin Jackson Architects
07050 097561
Pages **23ar, 69 both.**

**Gloss Ltd, Designers of
home accessories**
274 Portobello Road
London W10 5TE
020 8960 4146
pascale@
glossltd.u-net.com
Pages **74ac, 74bc, 97bc.**

**Greg Yale Landscape
Illumination**
27 Henry Road
Southampton
New York, NY 11968, USA
+ 1 516 287 2312
Page **100al.**

Guy Hills, Photographer
020 7916 2610
07831 548 068
guyhills@hotmail.com
Back jacket right, pages
15, 79bl.

Guy Stansfeld
020 7727 0133
Page **58bl.**

Henri Fitzwilliam-Lay
Interior design
hfitz@hotmail.com
Page **83bl.**

her house
30d Great Sutton Street
London EC1V 0DS
020 7689 0606/0808
www.herhouse.uk.com
Pages **48a, 115al.**

Het Grote Avontuur
Haarlemmerstraat 25
1013 EJ Amsterdam
The Netherlands
+ 31 (0)20 6268597
www.hetgroteavontuur.nl
Page **38.**

Helen Ellery
The Plot London
Interior Design
73 Compton Street
London EC1V 0BN
07974 173026
helen@helenellery.com
Pages **26b, 30, 33al, 46b
both, 47br.**

Hogarth Architects
(formerly Littman Goddard
Hogarth Architects)
61 Courtfield Gardens
London SW5 0NQ
020 7565 8366
www.hogartharchitects.
co.uk
Pages **76, 79al.**

Ian Chee
VX design & architecture
www.vxdesign.com
Pages **61br, 71br.**

Imogen Chappel
07803 156081
Page **115b.**

Interior Concepts
6 Warren Hall
Manor Road, Loughton
Essex IG10 4RP
020 8508 9952
0779 630 5133
www.jointeriorconcepts.
co.uk
Front jacket below left,
pages **27ar, 50–51.**

Jackson's
5 All Saints Road
London W11 1HA
020 7792 8336
Page **63ac.**

Janie Jackson,
Stylist/Designer
Parma Lilac
Children's nursery furniture
and accessories.
020 8960 9239
Pages **64, 66al, 106–107a.**

**Joanna Rippon and Maria
Speake, Retrouvius
Reclamation and Design**
32 York House
Upper Montagu Street
London W1H 1FR
020 7724 3387
07778 210855
Back jacket right, pages
15, 79bl.

Johanne Riss
35 Place du Nouveau
Marché aux Graens
1000 Brussels
Belgium
+ 32 2 513 0900
www.johanneriss.com
Page **78br.**

John Barman, Interior
design and decoration
500 Park Avenue
New York, NY 10022, USA
+1 212 838 9443
www.johnbarman.com
Page **67ar.**

Johnson Naylor
13 Britton Street
London EC1M 5SX
020 7490 8885
www.johnsonaylor.co.uk
Pages **80–81, 110br.**

Johnson Schwinghammer
335 West 38th Street # 9
New York, NY 10018, USA
+ 1 212 643 1552
www.jslighting.com
Pages **98, 101br.**

Jonathan Clark Architects
020 7286 5676
jonathan@jonathanclark
architects.co.uk
Pages **18l, 20bl, 26–27a.**

Jonathan Reed
Reed Creative Services
151a Sydney Street
London SW3 6NT
020 7565 0066
Page **73ar.**

Josephine Macrander
Interior designer
+ 31 299 402804
Page **35b.**

Just Design
80 Fifth Avenue, 18th Floor
New York, NY 10011, USA
+ 1 212 243 6544
wbp@angel.net
Page **67bl.**

Ken Foreman, Architect
105 Duane Street
New York, NY 10007, USA
+ 1 212 924 4503
Pages **2–3.**

Kristiina Ratia Designs
+ 1 203 852 0027
Front jacket centre; pages
11, 77, 79br, 84–85.

Lena Proudlock
25a Long Street, Tetbury
Gloucestershire GL8 8AA
www.deniminstyle.com
Pages **24–25b, 62bl.**

Lisa Bynon Garden Design
PO Box 897
Sag Harbor, NY 11963, USA
+ 1 631 725 4680
Pages **27br, 81b.**

Lloyd Schwan/Design
195 Chrystie Street, # 908
New York, NY 10002, USA
+1 212 375 0858
lloydschwan@earthlink.net
Pages **17ar, 24l, 28–29.**

Louise Robbins
Insideout House, Garden
Agency, Malt House B&B
Malt House, Almeley
Herefordshire HR3 6PY
01544 340681
www.insideout-
house&garden.co.uk
Pages **12–13, 39a, 104br.**

Lucy Salem
020 8563 2625
lucyandmarcsalem@
hotmail.com
*Makes and sources soft
furnishings and decorative
items for the home.*
Page **90a.**

**Mariette Himes Gomez
Associates, Inc.**
Interior decoration
504–506 East 74th Street
New York, NY 10021, USA
+1 212 288 6856
gomezny@ibm.net
Page **20al.**

**Mark Pynn AIA, McMillen
Pynn Architecture LLP**
PO Box 1068
Sun Valley, ID 83353, USA
+ 1 208 622 4656
www.sunvalleyachitect.com
Pages **60, 107bl.**

Mark Smith at Smithcreative
15 St Georges Road
London W4 1AU
020 8747 3909
mark@smithcreative.net
Page **52ar.**

Michael Benevento
Orange Group
515 Broadway
New York, NY 10012, USA
+ 1 212 965 8617
Page **84al.**

Michael Nathenson
Unique Environments
design & architecture
33 Florence Street
London N1 2FW
020 7431 6978
www.unique-environments.
co.uk
Front jacket above right.

Modernity
Köpmangatan 3
111 31 Stockholm, Sweden
+ 46 8 20 80 25
www.modernity.se
Page **23bl.**

The Moderns
900 Broadway
Suite 903
New York, NY 10003, USA
+ 1 212 387 8852
moderns@aol.com
Pages **4br, 112al.**

Mona Nerenberg
Bloom
43 Madison Street
Sag Harbor, NY 11963, USA
+ 1 631 725 4680
*Home and garden products
and antiques.*
Pages **27br, 81b.**

MOOArc
www.mooarc.com
Page **40al.**

Mullman Seidman Architects
Architecture and interior
design
443 Greenwich Street, # 2A
New York, NY 10013, USA
+ 1 212 431 0770
msa@mullmanseidman.com
Pages **17br, 20al, 71al.**

Nico Rensch
Architeam
www.architeam.co.uk
Pages **19br, 37ar, 82b.**

Ory Gomez
Didier Gomez
Interior Designer
15 rue Henri Heine
75016 Paris, France
+ 33 01 44 30 8823
orygomez@free.fr
Pages **78ar, 83ar.**

Project Orange
1st Floor
Morelands
7 Old Street
London EC1V 9HL
020 7689 3456
www.projectorange.com
Page **48b.**

R.K. Alliston
173 New Kings Road,
London SW6 4SW
and 6 Quiet Street
Bath BA1 2JS
+ 1 212 387 8852
www.rkalliston.com
mail order: 0845 130 5577
international line:
020 7751 0077
Pages **74–75.**

Paul Daly Design Studio
11 Hoxton Square
London N1 6NU
020 7613 4855
www.pauldaly.com
Pages **5b, 70a.**

Piero Castellini, Architect
Via della Rocca 5, MI, Italy
+ 39 02 48005384
studiocastellini@libero.it
Page **100r.**

Roger Oates Design
Rugs and Runners mail
order catalogue:
01531 631611
www.rogeroates.co.uk
Page **28al.**

SAD
07930 626916
sad@flymedia.co.uk
Page **112ar.**

Sage and Coombe Architects
(formerly Sage Wimer
Coombe Architects)
205 Hudson Street
Suite 1002
New York, NY 10013, USA
+ 1 212 226 9600
www.sageandcoombe.com
Pages **25br, 78bl, 90b.**

Sally Storey
John Cullen Lighting
020 7371 5400
Page **73ar.**

Sasha Waddell
269 Wandsworth Bridge Rd
London SW6 2TX
020 7736 0766
Page **29br.**

Sequana
64 Avenue de la Motte
Picquet
75015 Paris, France
+ 33 1 45 66 58 40
sequana@wanadoo.fr
Pages **75br, 107bc.**

Sergission Bates
44 Newman Street
London W1P 3PA
020 7255 1564
Page **73al.**

Seth Stein, Architect
15 Grand Union Centre
West Row
Ladbroke Grove
London W10 5AS
020 8968 8581
Pages **56l, 88al.**

**Shelton, Mindel &
Associates**
216 18th Street
New York, NY 10011, USA
+ 1 212 243 3939
Pages **98, 101br**

Sheppard Day Design
020 7821 2002
Front jacket below right,
pages **16ar, 22b.**

**Stickland Coombe
Architecture**
258 Lavender Hill
London SW11 1LJ
020 7924 1699
nick@scadesign.
freeserve.co.uk
Page **57bl.**

Steven Learner Studio
307 Seventh Avenue
Room 603
New York, NY 10001, USA
+ 1 212 741 8583
www.stevenlearner
studio.com
Page **83al.**

Studio Aandacht
Art direction and interior
production
www.studioaandacht.nl
Page **89bl.**

Studio Works
6775 Centinela Avenue
Building # 3
Culver City, CA 90230, USA
+ 1 301 390 5051
Page **71bl.**

Tito Canella Milan
Via Revere # 7/9
20123 Milan, Italy
+ 39 024695222
www.canella-achilli.com
Pages **5c, 26al, 32ar, 68,
115ar.**

www.tobiasjacobsen.dk
Pages **20–21.**

Totem Design, Ian Hume
2 Alexander Street
London W2 5NT
020 7243 0692
totem.uk@virgin.net
Page **83bl.**

Urban Salon
020 7357 8800
Pages **32br.**

USE Architects
11 Northburgh Street
London EC1V 0AH
020 7251 5559
use.arch@virgin.net
Page **66b.**

Vanessa Arbuthnott
Vanessa Arbuthnott Fabrics
The Tallet, Calmsden
Cirencester GL7 5ET
www.vanessaarbuthnott.
co.uk
Holiday lets:
www.thetallet.co.uk
Pages **28ac, 114.**

Vicente Wolf Associates
333 West 39th Street
New York, NY 10018, USA
www.vicentewolf
associates.com
+ 1 212 465 0590
Page **37l.**

**Vivien Lawrence Interior
Design**
Interior designer of private
homes
020 8209 0058/0562
vl-interiordesign@cwcom.net
Pages **49al, 56br.**

Voon Wong & Benson Saw
(formerly Voon Wong
Architects)
Unit 27, 1 Stannary Street
London SE11 4AD
020 7587 0116
www.voon-benson.co.uk
Pages **45, 49bl.**

Wallensteen & Co aab
Architect and design
consultants
Floragatan 11
114 31 Stockholm, Sweden
+ 46 8 210151
wallensteen@chello.se
Page **18br.**

William Yeoward
270 Kings Road
London SW3 5AW
020 7349 7828
www.williamyeoward.com
Pages **47al, 75cl.**

Woolf Architects
020 7428 9500
Page **27bl.**

Zina Glazebrook
ZG Design
Bridgehampton, New York
+ 1 631 537 4454
www.zgdesign.com
Back jacket centre.

index